Christian *Arts & Crafts*

VOLUME ONE

Mari González • Adell Harvey

Abingdon Press

CHRISTIAN ARTS AND CRAFTS
VOLUME 1

ISBN 0-687-07020-1

MANUFACTURED IN THE UNITED STATES OF AMERICA

To Grandma Farley,
who opened up
my world of crafts and creativity

—Mari

Ditto the above, from a daughter-in-law
who will be eternally
grateful for the hours that gracious lady
spent teaching her granddaughters
all those skills that I, the mother,
lacked.

—Adell

CONTENTS

Note: Asterisks beside each craft indicate that craft's level of difficulty—
* easy, ** moderate, *** difficult.

Introduction

You've been in them—the homes that are so cozy and warm they practically cry out to you to come in and put your feet up. They're bursting with the personality of the families they shelter.

No doubt you've been in the other ones, too—the ones that are so impersonal, so museum-like, you hardly dare breathe. Then there are the ones that lack just that extra touch, that spark that makes a well-dressed house a home.

Just as houses portray the love and warmth of their families so do churches testify to the personality of their congregations. Our country is littered with the impersonal mausoleums that double as "houses of worship" and the utilitarian buildings where people who are always on the run find an hour to give to God each week. Though fewer in number, there also are churches that exude the warmth and welcome of their congregations. They're the ones that make any visitor feel right at home.

What makes the difference? It's not money. Some of the wealthiest congregations in the country worship in the most impersonal of churches. And some of the poorest congregations learn of God in buildings filled with the signs of their love.

A big part is attitude. A church made up of loving, caring people who have the time and desire to reach into their community with God's love will be more inviting—more vibrant—than a church of worshipers who attend services out of habit or to fulfill a weekly obligation.

Another part of it is encouraging the members to use their God-given talents for the Lord.

You might be one of those people who get tongue-tied when faced with a room full of Sunday school students, who can't carry a tune even in the shower, or who dropped out of piano lessons after almost mastering the C scale. So what? Moses was like that and God still used him.

Instead of thinking about what you can't do, think about what you enjoy doing as hobbies or at work. Those crafts you create, that terrific sewing you do, those artful flower arrangements or drawings spring form talents that God wants you to use for him. They could provide just that touch to warm up your church. They could encourage a discouraged friend, perk up a tired missionary, or spread God's love to someone in your community.

Christian Arts and Crafts *is an idea book for putting your talents to God's use. Included in these pages are original craft ideas ranging from traditional basket weaving to crocheting, sewing, and macrame. Besides giving the biblical basis for glorifying God with crafts, it gives ideas on how to use craft projects to decorate the sanctuary, sell at Bazaars, and give as gifts.*

Whether you're an artisan, hobbyist, or a novice at crafts, there's a project in here for you. All it takes to turn your talents over to God are some ideas, a little skill, lots of patience, and—time.

There is one word to the wise. Though no one should discourage you from using your talents for God, do follow the protocol of your church. In some congregations, a sanctuary committee is set up to decide matters of decor. Other churches have the pastor, the elders, or women's group handle such things. And in other churches, anyone is free to add whatever he likes to God's house. While it is best to follow protocol, don't let that keep you from making a gift for God.

The book of Ecclesiastes warns, "There is nothing new under the sun." (1:9) With that in mind, we thank all those congregations and crafters who have inspired many of our ides. Special thanks go to family members Virginia Farley and Rhonda Navarro, both of whom lent their own crafting expertise and ideas for this project.

CRAFTERS CALLED BY GOD

The stories of the Israelites escaping Egyptian slavery only to wander in a harsh wilderness for forty years fill Bible storybooks and Sunday school curriculum. And when told, those stories evoke pictures of the Israelites worshiping God in a makeshift tent, the tabernacle of the wilderness.

True, the tabernacle was the center of worship for the children of Israel during their wilderness wanderings. And it was a tent. But the tabernacle was no makeshift, make-do, hurry-up-and-throw-it-together structure. Far from it. The tabernacle was designed by God himself.

The tabernacle was the only building ever constructed that was perfect from the beginning in every detail and never needed remodeling. When it came to craftsmanship, the tabernacle remains matchless to this day. It consisted of three tons of gold, five tons of silver, four tons of brass, and an assortment of jewels, fine wood, and fancy tapestries.

God gave its blueprint, pattern, and plan in minute detail to Moses, who entrusted its construction to a horde of escaped slaves.

While scripture devotes only two chapters to the creation of the universe, it uses more than forty chapters to describe in specific detail the tabernacle. This strong emphasis on the tabernacle marks it as vitally important. Volumes have been written to explain the tabernacle's theological significance.

Aside from all its rich spiritual truths, the tabernacle has much to offer from a purely practical standpoint.

In Exodus 25:2, God asked every person to give toward the tabernacle "willingly with his heart." These former slaves were to give freely of what they had in hand, from gold to goat hair. Even the least prosperous person had something to offer.

Likewise in today's churches, we have both rich and poor, people with much to give and people with little. Take Grandma June, for instance. To a stranger in the church, Grandma June probably doesn't seem like an important part of the congregation. She isn't the pastor, she doesn't teach Sunday school, she can't play the piano, and she'd never be asked to sing in the choir. Living on a fixed income, she doesn't have much to put in the offering plate as it passes by.

But like the freed slaves of Moses' day, Grandma June's devotion comes from a willing heart. The church building is filled with the outpouring of her talents. The church kitchen is equipped with her handmade potholders, embroidered dish towels, and curtains. The vacation Bible school crafts box spills over with her labors.

Grandma June's handiwork doesn't stop at the church doors; it turns up in the homes of every church member and any down-and-out family she can "adopt." Every baby born into that church is sure to be bundled up in a Grandma June quilt. Each little girl has a wardrobe of doll clothes crafted by the "church grandma," and each little boy has a wooden train made especially for him.

Frequently, Grandma June has wished aloud she could do more for the church. She's the first to say she has no talents, but she's wrong. Grandma June is no less a craftsperson than the principal workmen God endowed with "divine spirit, with ability, intelligence, and knowledge in every kind of craft" to make his tabernacle in the wilderness a place of great beauty and artistry.

When God called Bezalel to "devise artistic designs" for the tabernacle, he filled him with the "divine spirit with ability, intelligence, and knowledge in every kind of craft . . . in cutting of stones for setting, and in carving wood" (Exodus 31:2-5). Sounds like a modern-day craftsperson, doesn't he?

Later in Israel's history, King Solomon was called to build a temple to replace the temporary, portable tabernacle that had been the nation's place of worship for so long. King Solomon sent to Tyre and brought back Hiram, who was "full of skill, intelligence, and knowledge in working bronze" (I Kings 7:13).

In his dedicatory prayer, King Solomon stated the purpose for all the artistry and craftsmanship that went into the building of the temple: "So that all the peoples of the earth may know that the LORD is God; there is no other" (I Kings 8:60).

Has God given you a talent or skill to "make artistic designs?" Has he filled you with his Spirit in wisdom, in understanding, in knowledge, and in all kinds of craftsmanship?

Somewhere in your church is a spot that needs your particular style of creativity. Use your craftsmanship, not only to beautify your church, but to help "all the peoples of the earth to know that the LORD is God."

LIVENING UP THE WALLS

There was a time when most Protestant churches relied solely on architectural details, an attendance board, and a clock to break up the barren wall space stretching through the sanctuary. Fellowship halls got a little more relief with the typical portrait of Jesus. Sunday school classrooms were the brightest with charts, pictures, and maps tacked to the walls.

At long last, congregations are breaking away from that austere look, using banners, original paintings and murals, and other wall-hangings to both praise and honor God throughout the church building.

No matter what your craft, you can use it to liven up your church walls. Woodworkers can create sconces, wooden plaques, or intricate crosses as their contribution. The youth of the church can make original banners. Artists can couple the brush and inspiration for oil paintings, sketches, even murals. Crochet, appliqué, cross-stitch, etching, weaving, and quilting are all media that can be used to glorify God. And the list goes on.

***

Three Crosses • Crochet

Filet crochet is a simple type of crochet that produces a lacy silhouette by following a grid chart. It can be used to create wall-hangings, lacy lettered banners, quilt squares, table runners, or altar cloths. Any cross-stitch or grid pattern that relies on shape rather than color can be used for filet crochet.

The "Three Crosses" wall-hanging is great for Easter but could be used throughout the year. Since it is worked in a light thread, it looks best when hung against a dark surface such as dark paneling or a dark door.

SIZE: About 1 foot wide by 2 feet long.

MATERIALS: 1 big ball of cotton crochet thread (white or natural), medium weight; size 1 steel crochet hook; ¼-inch wooden dowel, 1 foot long; 2 wooden beads to fit on dowel; glue; wood stain; and cloth.

GAUGE: 7 double crochet equal 1 inch; 7 rows equal 2 inches.

DIRECTIONS: Chain (ch) 3, turn, at end of each row. Ch 3 counts as first double crochet (dc) of next row. Last dc of each row is worked into top of turning ch. Ch 56.

Row 1: Dc in 3rd ch from hook and in each ch across (55 dc). You have completed Row 1 of the chart, working from A to B across. Follow the chart beginning with Row 2. Work from B to A across. The beginning ch of each row is not shown on the chart. (For example, on Row 2, count the beginning ch as 1 dc and the 2 shaded squares as 4 dc for a total of 5 dc.) Work from A to B across all odd-numbered rows and B to A across the even-numbered rows. Complete 67 rows. At end, do not ch or end off.

Edging, Rnd 1: With right side facing, ch 1, single crochet (sc) in last dc worked. Turn work slightly. Working along long side, sc evenly down the side (2 sc in each dc). Work 3 sc in bottom corner. Continuing around short end, work sc in bottom of each of the next 53 dc. Work 3 sc in next dc (corner made). Using the same method, sc along remaining long side and the top. Join with slip stitch in first sc. Ch 1.

Rnd 2: Sc in first sc, *skip next sc, work 5 dc in next sc (shell made), skip next sc, sc in next sc (repeat from * all the way around both sides and the bottom, working a shell into each bottom corner). End at top with a sc in the top corner sc, sc in next sc, (ch 7, skip next sc, sc in each of next 3 sc) 13 times, ch 7, slip stitch into beginning ch. End off. Weave in loose ends.

Finishing: Stain dowel and wooden beads. Slip dowel through the chain loops at the top of hanging. To make hanging cord, ch 5. Slip stitch into beginning ch, ch 75. Do not end off. Slip 1 end of dowel through beginning loop of ch. Glue beads on both ends of dowel. Form loop on other end of dowel (between the last loop of the hanging and the wooden bead) by working 5 ch around dowel. Slip stitch into 75th ch. End off. Weave in loose ends.

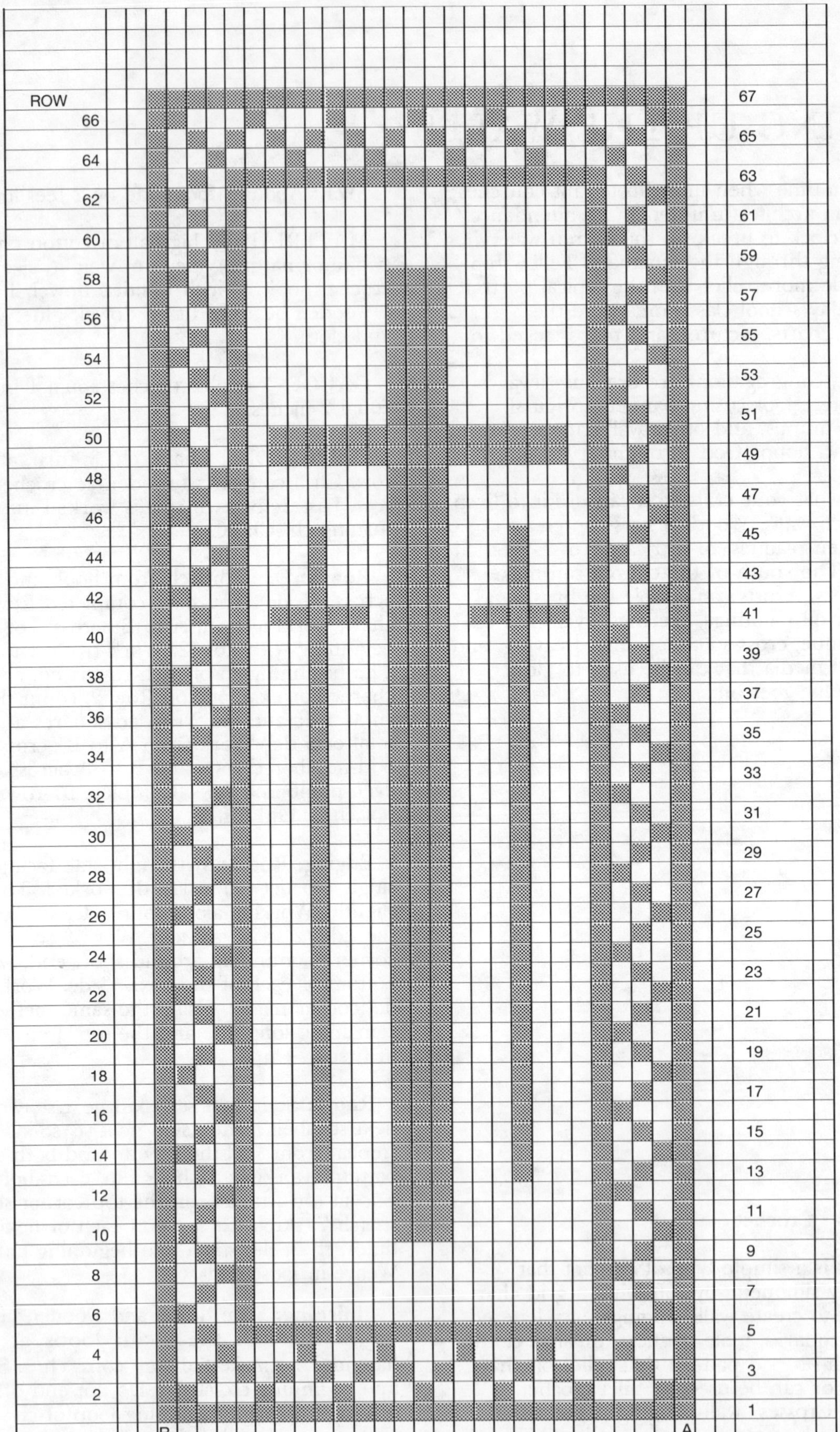

■ = 2 dc

□ = ch 1, sk 1 ch, dc in next dc

*

Rubbings • Art

England's churches and cemeteries abound with ancient brass memorials, depicting civil, religious, and military figures.

While it's impossible to adorn our own twenty-first century churches with such artistry, we can recapture the essence of the period by the simple process of brass rubbing, which is similar to the process children use when they rub a coin through paper by using a soft lead pencil. Rubbings make beautiful, unique wall hangings for a chapel or sanctuary.

Europe, of course, is the only place for Renaissance rubbings. If someone in your group is planning a vacation in London or Paris, encourage him to try his hand at it. Rubbing is so popular in London, many bookshops there sell pamphlets that list the locations of good brasses and materials needed to complete the job.

Though not of the Renaissance era, objects for rubbing can be found closer to home. Commemorative plaques, cemetery headstones, historical markers, and objects as common as old manhole covers make excellent subjects for rubbings.

MATERIALS: Lightweight, slightly textured paper, such as white poster paper, can be bought by the yard or the roll. Rice paper is another good choice, as it produces a rubbing of beautiful quality. In England, a special heelball is readily available. In the United States, use a chunk of black finishing wax, available at shoe repair stores. You'll also need masking tape and a soft cloth.

DIRECTIONS: Brush surface dirt off the brass with the soft cloth. Roll the paper over the brass, leaving extra at top, bottom, and sides to allow for framing. Secure paper with masking tape. With your finger, trace the outline of the object, making a slight indentation in the paper to use as a general guide.

Rubbing lightly at first with the finishing wax, slowly increase the pressure, always rubbing in the same direction. The darker you get the rubbing the better it will look, so maintain a steady pressure to ensure a consistent degree of blackness.

Make sure you have rubbed the entire brass. Go over any light areas, then lightly brush off excess wax. Carefully remove the masking tape. Your rubbing is ready to frame.

*

Wreaths • Craft

In the early days of America, country folk hung wreaths or bundles of wheat on their doors to signify that the harvest was finished and they were again ready to receive guests.

What a lovely way to let guests know they're welcome in our churches! A spray of grain tied with a bright bow and hung on the front door of the church would certainly add a cheery, welcoming note.

Wreaths are normally associated with Advent and Christmas, but they certainly are not limited to those seasons. Grapevine wreaths can be adorned with flowers or fruit to fit any seasonal decor. Grapevine wreaths come in a number of sizes and shapes at craft shops. If you have access to a vineyard, the wreaths are quite simple to make.

DIRECTIONS: Cut the vines after the grapes are gone in the fall. Twist the supple vines into a circle the size you want. Keep adding vines until the wreath is as thick as you desire. Fasten in place with florist wire.

For springtime, add spring flowers (daisies, pansies, etc.) and perhaps a bird's nest or a tiny bird on a flowering branch.

A summer wreath could be covered with roses and a bright bow or an assortment of wildflowers. In the fall, add nuts, a tiny squirrel or two, and autumn leaves.

And in winter, holly, mistletoe, tiny red bows or a big plaid bow, holiday picks, or tiny red poinsettias bring your grapevine into the season.

An all-season wreath can be made by loosely wrapping a variety of ribbons around the wreath and adding dried flowers or wooden miniatures to match your decor.

For an evergreen wreath, make a huge circle of chicken wire. Insert large pine branches, securing with hot glue and/or florist wire. Keep branches symmetrical. Fill in as needed. When your wreath is fully covered, add a strand of miniature white, gold, or blue Christmas lights and a large plastic bow. Hang the wreath on an outside wall of your church.

Straw wreaths, purchased from a craft store, can be wrapped in ribbon, decorated with flowers, or even covered with wrapped candies for use in the church kitchen. Use some of the wooden welcome signs, ducks, or animals available at craft stores to further decorate the wreath.

An unusual wreath can be made using a straw or foam form as a base and cornhusks or raffia for the cover. Fold small pieces of cornhusk in half and staple (or glue) to the wreath until the form is completely covered with the cornhusk "bows." Add country-style bows at intervals around the wreath for color or insert a flower or two.

For Christmas, add tiny gold musical instrument ornaments to a cornhusk wreath and hang it on the wall above the piano for a nice touch.

A bathroom wreath can be made by covering a foam form with a lush terrycloth towel and washcloth. This project is easier with two people but requires only a few minutes. Tightly stretch one long end of the towel to inside of wreath form. Using flat-headed straight pins, pin in place. Keeping taut, wrap towel tightly around wreath. When all wrapped, secure other long end out of sight with straight pins. If the towel didn't cover the entire form, cover the gap, in the same way, with a matching washcloth. Adorn with lace, ribbon, rickrack, sprigs of flowers, or whatever your imagination dictates.

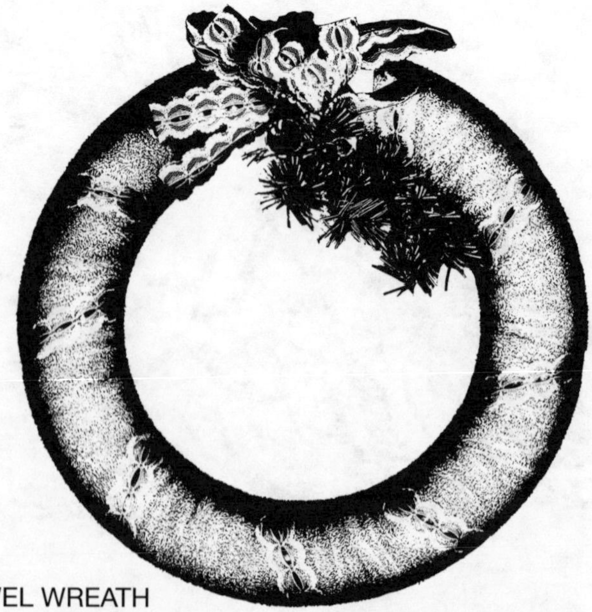

TERRYCLOTH TOWEL WREATH

CORNHUSK
WREATH

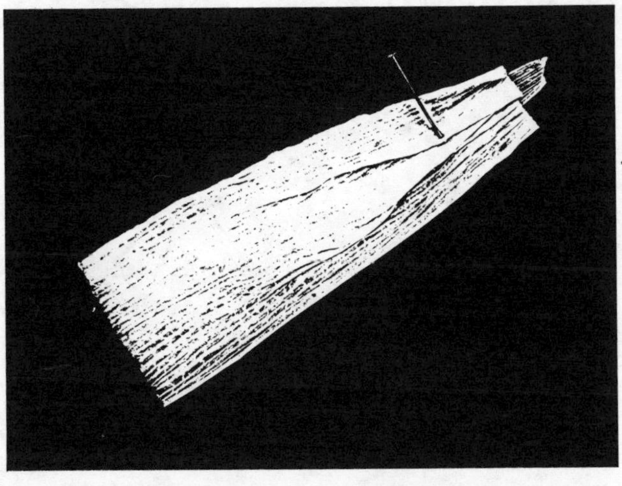

← CORNHUSK BOW

*

Wall Mats • Craft

A few picks of flowers, some ribbon, and just a little bit of time can turn a round wicker mat into a beautiful wall hanging for a hallway, bathroom, or fellowship hall. It can be changed with the seasons or for a mere switch of color.

MATERIALS: A round, woven wicker mat; half a craft foam ball or egg (size should be about the size of the center of mat); long piece of florist wire; 6-10 picks of silk flowers or seasonal flowers; 5 coordinating pipe cleaners; pencil; coordinating ribbon; glue gun; and long straight pins. The width of ribbon and the number of picks all depend on how large a mat you use.

DIRECTIONS: Place foam piece in front center of mat. Insert florist wire through back center of mat; wrap around foam tightly; bring end through to back again. Tightly twist the two ends of florist wire together; push flat against back of mat, trimming ends if necessary. Insert picks in foam, arranging and filling in evenly and for balance. Wrap each pipe cleaner tightly around a pencil. Pull out pencil and loosen spirals of pipe cleaner. Insert pipe cleaners evenly throughout arrangement. Weave ribbon through mat, about 1-3 inches from edge. Glue ends securely at back of mat. Make little bows from extra ribbon. Using straight pins, push bows into flower arrangement. Or make one large bow to glue to ribbon at center bottom of hanging.

For Valentine's Day, use picks of red flocked roses; white pipe cleaners; red calico, paisley, velvet, or satin craft ribbon.

A spring arrangement can be made with picks of baby blue silk roses; baby's breath; natural pipe cleaners; light blue satin ribbon edged with natural lace.

A summer arrangement would use picks of bright wildflowers with matching pipe cleaners and a calico craft ribbon that picks up the colors of the flowers.

For fall, use picks of autumn leaves, gold or burnt orange pipe cleaners, and an autumn calico craft ribbon. Novelty picks of pilgrims, turkeys, or fall vegetables could be added for a Thanksgiving theme.

Christmas is the easiest because of the large selection of holiday picks available. Use picks of pine cones, evergreen branches, little wrapped packages, or holly. Add coordinating pipe cleaners and a plaid ribbon with bits of metallic. Though red and green are the traditional Christmas colors, you don't have to limit yourself to that color theme. A lot of blues, mauves, and burgundies are making their way into the Christmas crafts selection.

Other looks can be made by adding novelty picks such as musical instruments or other miniatures.

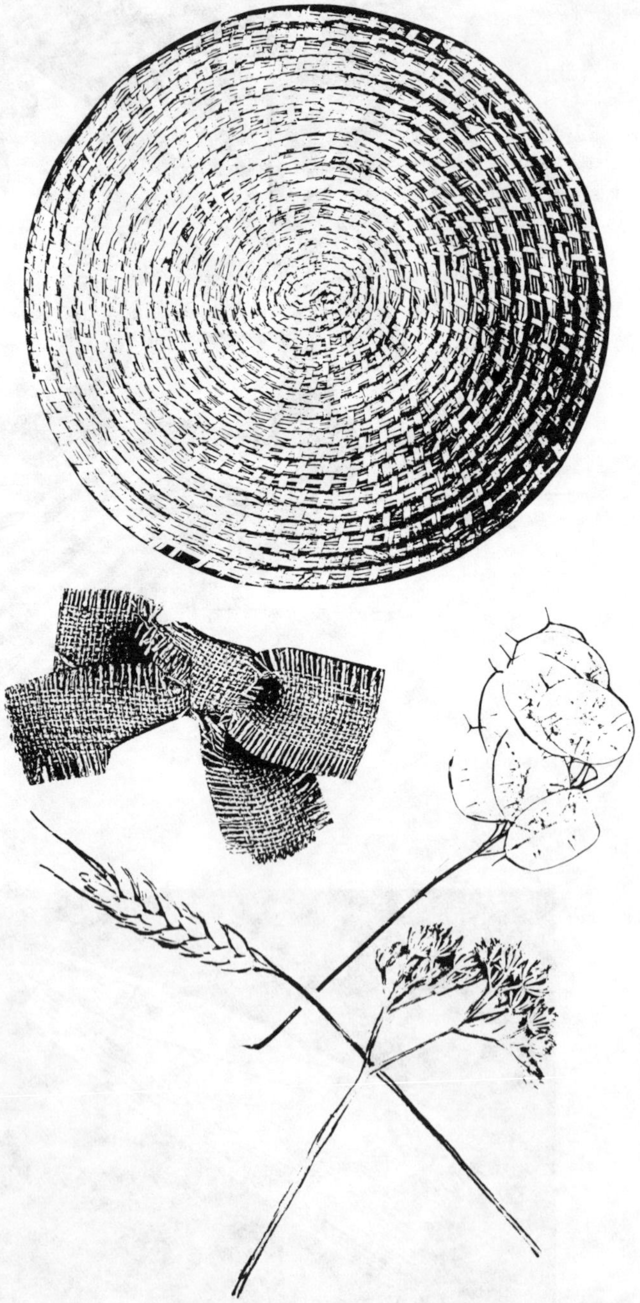

ADDING THE RIGHT TOUCH

When it comes to fashion or decorating, accessorizing makes all the difference in the world. Unfortunately, when it comes to churches, accessories are often overlooked or considered a nonessential.

Just as accessories can make a house a home, expressing the personality of the family that lives there, they can make a church far more than just a structure while expressing the personality of the congregation.

Accessories also offer the widest range of possibilities for the crafter, although they may require the most imagination.

One of the most common accessories found in a church is flower arrangements or potted plants at Easter and Christmas. Why not add to that with real greenery brightening up classrooms, the church library, the kitchen, and even the bathroom? A macrame plant hanger complements fresh greenery while adding that warm touch that says, "We care."

Baskets are another homey touch that can do wonders for a church if artfully arranged and used. One church in Wyoming used an assortment of handmade baskets and hand-thrown pottery on high shelves surrounding the walls of the sanctuary. Small loaves of homemade bread sealed with varnish tumbled from the baskets, evoking visions of the little boy who shared his lunch with the multitude that had gathered to meet Jesus.

Other accessories can include ornate picture frames, mirrors, a collection of old Bible story books or theological tomes, hand-dipped candles and an assortment of handmade candlesticks, original sculpture, wood carvings—the list is endless.

How you use the accessories is a test of your imagination and decorating skills. For starters, look at the church as if it were your home. Where are those homey touches needed? If it were a house, how would you decorate it? After all, the church is the house of God and his people.

BANNER

*

Flower Power

The foyer or narthex is designed especially to welcome church family, friends, and guests into the church. Set the stage for a grand welcome with an artful bouquet of flowers, greenery, or even fresh vegetables or fruit set on a low chest or table near the entrance.

Most of us have come to expect a floral arrangement on the altar table or piano in our churches. But there are dozens of churches whose front altars are absolutely bare. In most instances, the oversight is not intentional. Incredibly, some congregations simply never think to adorn their worship centers with God's creative handiwork.

Flowers need not be expensive arrangements purchased weekly from professional florists. Some of the simplest and most effective displays are wildflowers or garden varieties informally arranged in an attractive vase or bowl.

When selecting a container, consider the colors of the flowers that you plan to use. Green, white, and clear glass or crystal are good choices for any color bouquet. Cattails and dried weeds look great in brown pottery or natural baskets. Brilliant orange calendulas in a cornflower blue vase would be stunning. Pink roses or carnations are at their loveliest when arranged in a deep cranberry glass vase.

Keep flowers and containers consistent in texture as well. Small, fragile flowers should be paired with delicate containers such as crystal or glass.

DIRECTIONS: Begin by wedging well-soaked florist foam into the container, strapping it down with florist tape. For large arrangements, the foam should extend one or two inches above the top of the container, so branches can be anchored at angles to create graceful, down-sweeping lines.

Select an assortment of greenery, such as holly, croton leaves, pine, fern, hemlock, magnolia, or whatever is seasonably available. Cut stems at an angle to allow the most moisture to be absorbed.

To artfully arrange a bouquet, anchor the largest branches in the container to establish basic lines of a design. Depending on the container and the available space, the basic outline can be rounded, fanlike, A-frame, or triangular.

Insert additional foliage to fill in the basic outline, establishing the beginning of a focal point. Add blooms, berries, or vegetables to give color and to further fill in.

Make certain greenery extends upward, forward, and out on either side to keep the design balanced and looking good from three sides.

For Japanese-style formal arrangements, simplicity is the key. "Better too few than too many" is the credo of master Japanese flower designers.

Begin a large arrangement with three stalks of flowers, such as gladiola, snapdragons, lilies, or larkspur. Cut the tallest stalk to 1½ times the diameter of the bowl, the second to ⅔ the height of the first, and the third about ½ or ⅓ the height of the second. In an Oriental arrangement, these three stalks are referred to as "heaven, man, and earth."

Impale the three stalks on a pinpoint holder or in the florist foam. Add a few smaller blooms or greens to soften the effect.

If you replace the water in the container daily, arrangements will stay fresh for a week to ten days.

Silk and dried flowers are so abundant these days that no church need ever be without altar and foyer flowers. To keep expenses down, pick up bundles of silk flowers at garage sales, flea markets, and close-out sales. Keep them in large boxes by color and arrange them as you would fresh flowers.

Because the artificial varieties need no water, there's no limit to the type of containers you can arrange them in. An interesting piece of driftwood can become a piece of art when silk flowers are attached to it in strategic places.

For an unusual altar table arrangement, use candles and a large family Bible unified by a fabric drape tossed informally on the table. Strew color-matched silk flowers and baby's breath around the arrangement.

For Thanksgiving, use a cornucopia filled with fresh or wax fruit, a gold drape, autumn candles, and silk autumn leaves for a striking effect. To add height to one of the elements, place a small box under it and cover the box casually with the drape.

***

Domed Plant Hanger • Macrame

Although it is intricate, macrame is also a quick craft that can produce useful and beautiful accessories for the home or church. Plant hangers are probably the most common macrame projects, but macramed wall-hangings, window coverings, and utensil holders could also be used in the church.

While macrame consists of simple knots, it gets its unique look from the beads, rings, and cord you choose to use. All of these can be coordinated to fit into just the right niche in the church.

MATERIALS: 620 yards 5-millimeter cord; two 12-inch wooden rings; an 18-inch wooden ring; a 2-inch metal ring; a 6-inch metal ring; eight 2-inch long wooden or ceramic beads; glue gun; paint or stain for wooden beads.

DIRECTIONS: Cut cord into proper lengths. You will need seventy-two 5-yard lengths; seventy-two 3-yard lengths; four 7-yard lengths, four 2-yard lengths; and two ½-yard lengths.

Dome Top: Fold the 5-yard cords in half. Place on a 12-inch ring with a larks head (lh) knot. Divide cords into 36 groups of 4 each. Tie a square knot (sk) with each group of 4 cords directly below the lh. Alternate cords and tie another row of sk. Do this 9 more times for a total of 11 rows. Double half hitch (dhh) the ends of cords onto the 18-inch wooden ring. Trim the ends to the desired length for fringe and brush out.

Plant Holder Bottom: Fold the 3-yard cords in half. Attach 12-inch ring, using a lh. Divide cords into 36 groups of 4 each. Tie a sk with each group of 4 directly below the lh. Alternate cords and tie another row of sk. Repeat 4 more times for a total of 6 rows. Dhh the ends of cord to the 6-inch metal ring. Trim ends to the desired length for fringe and brush out.

Middle: If using wooden beads, paint or stain them.

On dome top, divide knots around the 12-inch wooden ring into 4 equal groups. Fold the 2-yard cords in half; lh onto wooden ring between each of the 4 sections of the dome top. Fold the 7-yard cords in half; lh over the top of each of the 2-yard lengths, placing the longer cords on the outside. With each group of 4 cords, half knot twist sinnet with the outer cords down ⅓ the length of the cord, using the 2-yard cords as filler. Thread a bead on the two middle cords and slide up to end of work. Continue half knot twist sinnet for the same length as before. Thread on another bead. Half knot twist sinnet the rest of the length of the cords.

On planter bottom, divide the knots around the wooden ring into 4 equal groups. Tie the 4 completed middle cords onto the wooden ring between each of the 4 sections. Secure ends by cutting close to the knot. With a hot glue gun, carefully glue ends down.

Finishing: Lh ½-yard cords onto the 2-inch metal ring. Separate the knotted cords at the top of the dome into 4 even groups. With glue gun, glue the 4 ends of the ½-yard cords onto the wooden top ring, 1 end between each group of knots. Allow the glue to cool before hanging planter.

Baskets • Craft

In a tradition as old as America, many people are rediscovering the relaxing, exhilarating craft of basket weaving.

There's something in a hand-woven basket that we all respond to—an aura of creativity, of simple use, a strong sense of the person who made it. A basket full of wildflowers set on an altar, piano, or in the foyer of a church gives a sense of timelessness and brings nature into the setting.

Baskets also can be used as wall hangings in bathrooms, nurseries, or conference rooms and as excellent bazaar crafts (filled with jams and jellies, holiday goodies, decorative soaps, tiny toys, costume jewelry, wool and yarn, tea, spices, espresso coffees, potpourri, fruit, napkins, what have you—they sell out quickly at bazaar tables).

Baskets personalized for special occasions make excellent group gifts for weddings, bridal or baby showers, or for guest speakers. For a kitchen shower, you may want to fill a basket with kitchen tools and gadgets; a basket loaded with bath sponges, colognes, powders, and other bath luxuries could be a centerpiece for a bridal luncheon. A nice wedding basket for a couple leaving on a honeymoon is filled with crackers, cheese, pepperoni, nuts, and other snack foods for munching along the way.

Most craft stores offer basket-making classes and sell the rattan reed, seaweed, and other materials. Part of the enjoyment for some basket makers, however, is foraging for natural grasses and vines. A few stalks from redbuds along the roads, cattails, the suckers that grow around chokecherry bushes, or the tender shoots or whips that are pruned from apple, plum, and pear trees make lovely baskets.

More energetic basketmakers weave their baskets from splints, flexible strips of wood from the trunks of ash, oak, hickory, and maple trees. This requires hammering a debarked log with a heavy mallet to loosen strips of wood or quartering a small log and using a wedge (called a froe) to shave sections into splints.

Anything pliable can be used as weavers—from horsehair to grapevines and willow, to baling twine or fabric cording. People who forage from nature for their materials should remember to leave plenty of growth for next year to conserve our resources. Bark should be peeled from saplings in small, vertical sections to allow the tree a healthy recovery.

***

Egg Basket • Craft

TOOLS: Tape measure, awl or ice pick, needle-nose pliers, water basin (a large dishpan or plastic bucket works nicely), spring-type clothespins, cutting tool.

MATERIALS: One 8-inch hoop, one hank of No. 7 round reed for spokes and handle, one hank of ¼-inch flat reed. (Note: The smallest hanks come in one-pound sizes, so you should have enough for two or more baskets.) For the first rows of weaving, some people prefer to use a No. 2 round reed; others split the ¼-inch flat reed in half lengthwise for a tighter basket.

Rattan reed is sold in coils or hanks—hanks are generally preferred because you can see what you are getting. Look for reed that is not "hairy" or split. For colored baskets, reed can be dyed by dipping in regular clothing dye. More expensive basket dye is available at craft shops. Reed can also be dyed naturally, using things like walnut shells, which give the rattan a nice brown color. For color-matched hues, simply dunk the reed in the water used to wash out paint brushes after a decorating project or use wood stains thinned with paint thinner.

DIRECTIONS: Select the 2 longest pieces of flat reed from the hank, preferably 9-10 feet long, but not less than 8 feet in length. Place them in warm water for 5-10 minutes or until the reed is flexible. Also soak 2 long strands of small round reed or split flat reed, whichever you plan to use for the first round of weaving.

Meanwhile, cut a piece of the No. 7 round reed about the same circumference as your hoop. Place it upright inside the hoop, centering it for the basket handle and bottom spoke. Make certain the open ends of the reed come together where the handle intersects the rim hoop and secure temporarily with a clothespin. (Some basketmakers prefer to use a second hoop identical to the rim instead of the round reed for a basket handle.)

Beginning with a woven "X" at this spot, weave a god's eye with the long flat reed, securing the rim to the handle. To begin the 4-point lashing of the god's eye, place one tip end of the reed smooth side up, pointing up to the left. Bring the reed under the arm of the ring at 6 o'clock, diagonally up over the ring at 3 o'clock, then down under it.

Continue wrapping counterclockwise, rotating the basket clockwise so the ring arm you are wrapping around is always at 3 o'clock. Wrap over, back under, and over again around each of the 4 arms of the rings, keeping the tension tight until that reed is used. Be careful not to overlap, checking the inside of the basket to make sure the weaver doesn't overlap where it goes around the rings.

With an awl, tuck the end of the reed back underneath the god's eye. If the end slips out when the reed has dried, a dab of glue and a clothespin to hold it in place while it dries will come to the rescue.

Using the second length of flat reed, make an identical god's eye on the other side.

While making the god's eyes, put 10-12 more strands of flat reed to soak. From the No. 7 round reed, cut two 14-inch spokes (ribs) with a sharp slant toward the inside of the natural curve, leaving the ends sharp to insert inside the god's eye. Place the cut end into the center of the lashing shoulder, pointing the slanted part toward the inside of the basket. This becomes the pivotal rib. Bend the rib and insert it in the opposite god's eye.

Cut more ribs and place them on both sides of the pivotal rib in a shape that you like. Cut identical ribs for the opposite side for uniformity. Nestle the ribs snugly into the lashing shoulder, but don't cram them.

Continue cutting and inserting spokes, graduating their sizes to make the framework for the basket. You should have no more than a 2-finger width between spokes for a nice, tight basket, which means you'll have about 6-7 ribs per side. When you are satisfied with the shape and size of your framework, secure the spokes with clothespins and begin weaving.

Using one strand of the damp, split flat reed or the No. 2 round reed, begin weaving beneath the god's eye on one side. With the basket upside-down, begin on the right and anchor the end by passing the weaver under the rim, over the first rib, and under the second. Slip the end down to hide it beneath the lashing. Push the reed up tight against the last weaving row. Weave over one, under one, including the rims and bottom of the handle ring. Leave the end of your weaver hanging to overlap when you add a new weaver.

Use an identical length on the other side, then begin weaving with the ¼-inch flat reed. If you are using different colored reeds, be sure to keep the lengths identical on each side for a balanced look. Avoid twisting the weaver and feed it where it exits and enters over and under the ribs, rather than weaving with the free end of the weaver.

To achieve a balanced shape, weave both sides simultaneously, trying not to get more than 6-8 rows ahead on either side. Keep weaving tension the same from right to left as from left to right; otherwise the basket will have a corrugated effect with alternate ribs riding higher.

After weaving 8-10 rows on each side, add

additional ribs as needed, keeping both sides of the baskets balanced in number. Slide the new rib down alongside each original rib to the rim side of that rib, making sure it is under no more than 4 rows of weaving.

Add a new weaver when necessary. End the short weaver on top of a spoke and overlap the last 4 spokes with a new weaver and continue weaving. As the rows of weaving get nearer the center or bottom of the basket, fill in the buttocks with an elliptical shape. Weaving from the rim toward the basket bottom, go 1 rib past the longest or pivotal rib. Turn around on this rib and weave to the rib on the other side of the pivotal rib (over 1, under 1). Turn around on this rib, encompassing 3 ribs.

Continue in this manner, increasing the fill by 1 rib each time, until you have turned around on every rib on the side of the buttocks on which you are working. Never turn around on the bottom of the handle ring.

When you reach this point, continue weaving across to the rim of the opposite buttock and repeat, increasing the fill on that side.

When the basket is completely woven, protect it by brushing on a coat of oil.

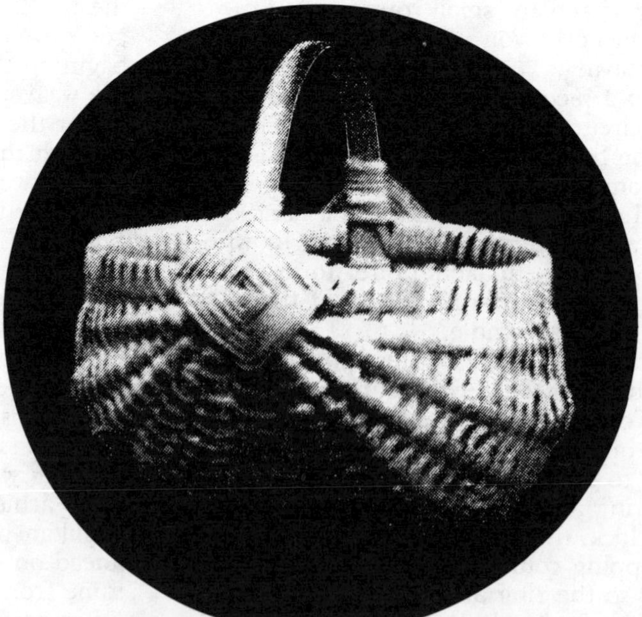

EGG BASKET

DIAGRAMS FOR EGG BASKET

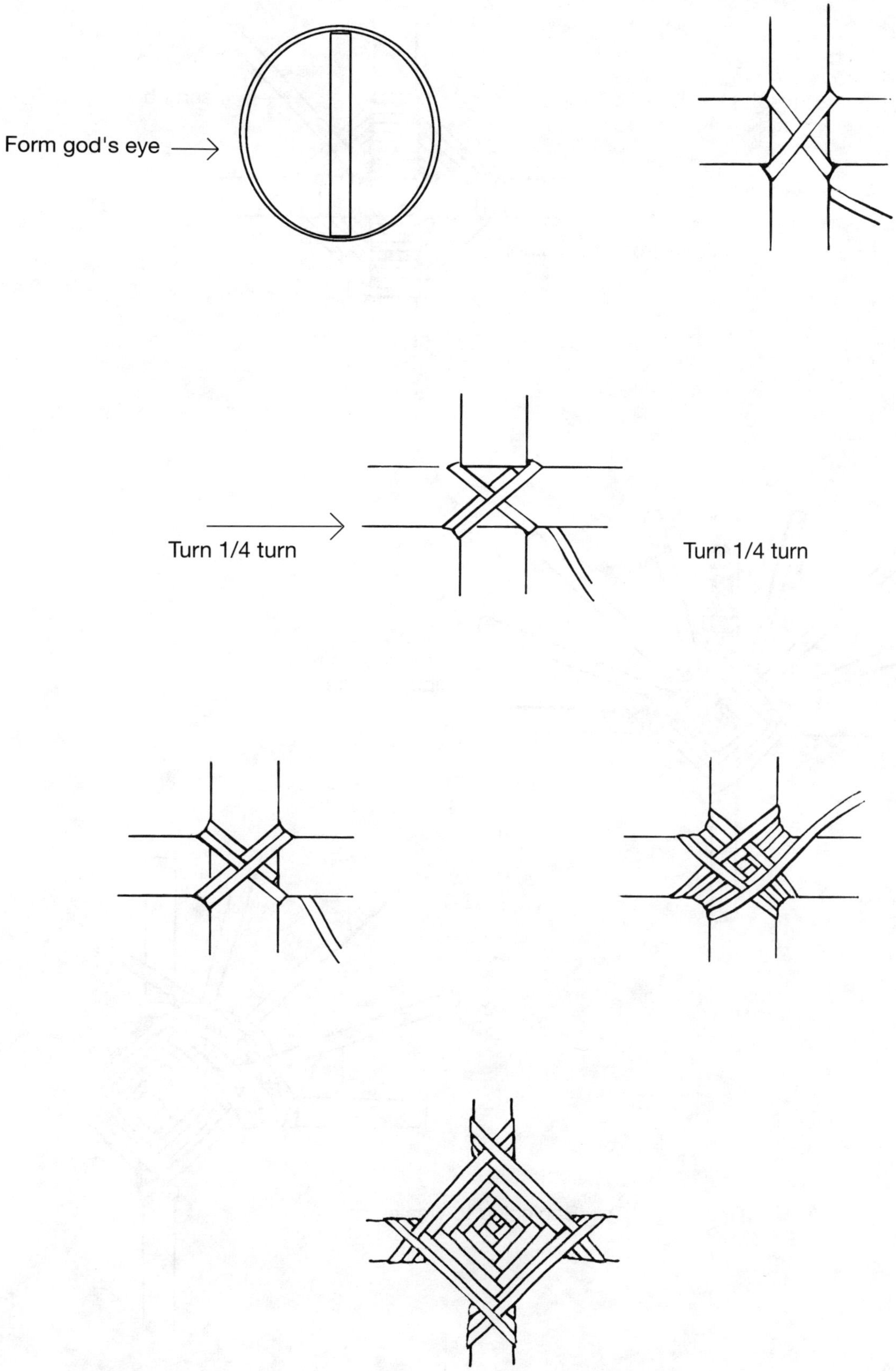

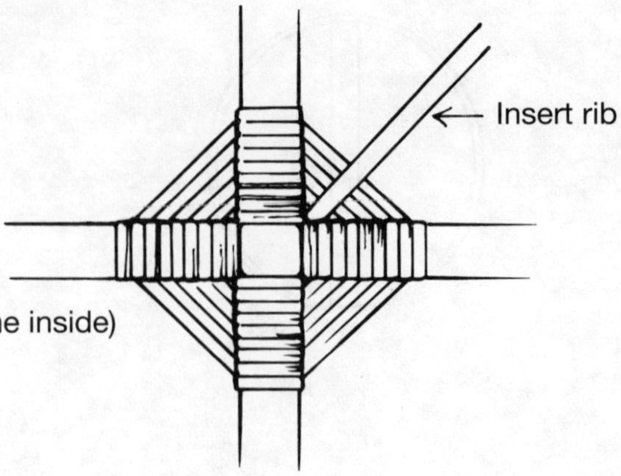

(View from the inside)

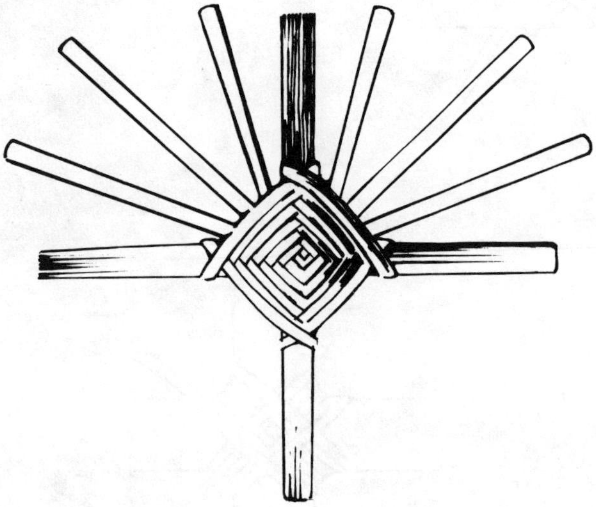

Ribs in place

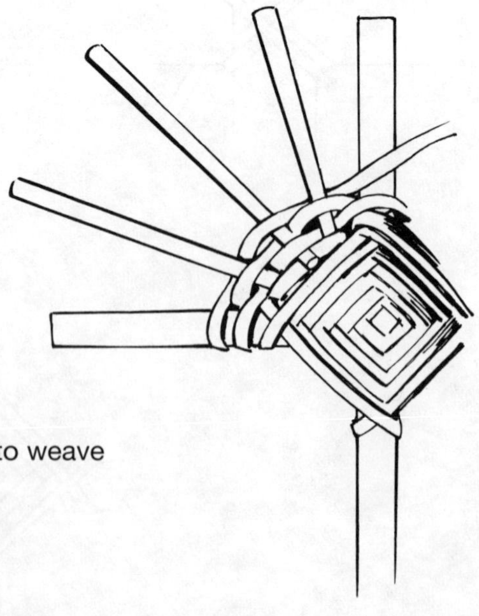

Beginning to weave

*

Frames • Craft

"A little dab will do you" is never more true than when using paint to cover up the ravages of time. Many churches have lovely old tapestries or paintings that could be renewed with better frames, but complementary frames would cost more than the wall-hanging is worth.

That's when faux painting comes to the rescue. Existing frames or frames picked up cheaply at garage or estate sales can be made to mimic elegant tortoiseshell veneer with surprisingly little effort. With swirls and streaks of brown and gold, your frame will closely resemble original tortoiseshell, which is made from thin layers of the shell of the hawksbill tortoise.

MATERIALS: Gold spray paint; varnish stain in old maple, antique walnut, and tudor shades; paint thinner; glossy varnish; and artist's brushes.

DIRECTIONS: Sand the old frame, smoothing all rough spots. Rub with a cloth dipped in paint thinner to remove all dirt and dust.

Spray the frame with several thin layers of gold spray paint, allowing the base coat to dry completely before applying next layer. Use short, quick strokes so the paint doesn't run.

When paint is thoroughly dry, brush on a solid coat of varnish stain. While it is still wet, brush, dab, or drip on additional colors. The first color used will be the major color, with subtle shadings created by the order in which the other colors are used.

When the varnish starts to dry (about 5-10 minutes), apply paint thinner in the same manner you applied the varnish (dabbed, brushed, dripped, or sprayed lightly with an atomizer). The gold base coat will shine through and the varnish becomes darker around the edges wherever the thinner falls.

Different effects can be obtained by the length of your brush strokes. Short, diagonal strokes will give a subtler, less dramatic effect than would longer brush strokes.

When the piece is completely dry, protect your masterpiece with one or more coats of the glossy varnish.

CRAFTS IN THE CHURCH KITCHEN

The church kitchen, though well stocked, is often one of the drabbest places in God's house. Yet, it is one of the easiest rooms to spice up with a variety of crafts and some imagination.

A church kitchen is much like a home kitchen. It thrives on homey touches. Those touches warm up the kitchen while making it a pleasant place to work. The kitchen cries out for wall brighteners such as plaster plaques, stained-glass window hangings, country wreaths, hand-carved toweling, and spice racks. Macrame hangers can double for plants or utensil holders. Nice, large potholders and trivets are a necessity along with a variety of tablecloths and runners.

Craft books abound with kitchen decor that can be adapted for church kitchens. Many of them would make great projects for the youth of the church. Having some of their handiwork in the church will instill in them a sense of pride in the upkeep and appearance of the church. And it will let them know that this is their church, too.

Most books, though, don't have much for institutional kitchens. Since church kitchens and dining areas center around the table, that's where we'll start. Instead of toppling the budget for new tables, put your carpenters to work. Gang-sized tables can be made from hollow-core doors or sheets of plywood and a couple of folding table-leg assemblies purchased at discount hardware stores.

The foundation for the decor for all church potlucks and banquets is the tablecloth. A kitchen stocked with a variety of tablecloths makes decorating for special events much easier. Happy the banquet committee that has a linen closet filled with tablecloths and runners ranging from formal to casual and in a rainbow of hues at its disposal.

Lace tablecloths can be knitted or crocheted. Since such a project is a labor of love, it should only be undertaken as a gift to God as most non-crocheters or non-knitters cannot truly appreciate all the hours that go into it. If time is a factor, stick with lacy table runners.

The easiest tablecloths are ones stitched up from washable sheets or easy-care, but durable, fabric. Such cloths require little sewing ability, but careful measuring. Accessorizing with store-bought laces and trims or topping with runners, cloth napkins, placemats, and such can dress up a simple cloth.

An array of thick potholders and trivets made to coordinate with the tablecloths will protect the cloths while giving the dining area a put-together look rather than the disheveled appearance that it was stocked with everyone's cast-offs.

QUILTED TABLERUNNER

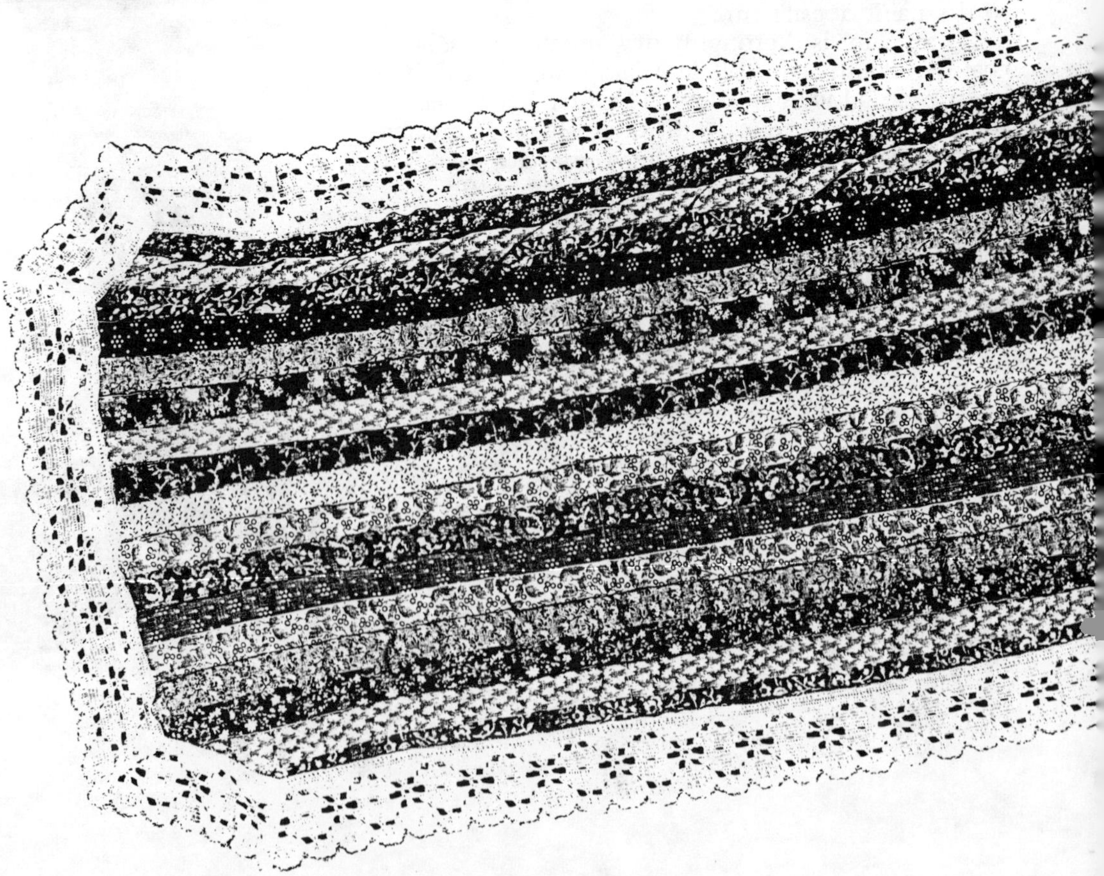

*

Tablecloths • Sewing

Before you can determine yardage, you need to carefully measure the width and length of the table. For a casual look, allow for a 6-inch drop. A 12-inch drop will give a more formal look. Allow an extra inch on each side for a narrow hem.

To figure fabric width, add the width measurement of your table plus 14 inches for a casual cloth or 26 inches for a dressier look. If your table is 30 inches wide, you will need fabric at least 44 inches wide for casual or 56 inches wide for formal. Most fabrics come in widths of 44/45 inches, 54 inches, or 60 inches. Bed sheets give ample width for tablecloths and are often cheaper than fabric. To make your job easier, avoid fabric widths that would require a seam.

Now, for length. Measure how long your table is. Add either 14 or 26 inches to that measurement. Divide by 36. That will tell you how many yards of fabric you need.

Before hemming the cloth, prewash your fabric and press. Trim away any excess from width. Save the scraps for napkin rings or pieced potholders and tablerunners.

To hem, use the seam guide on your sewing machine and stitch a line ½ inch from the edge all the way around the cloth. Fold along stitching; fold once more so raw edge is encased. Pin. Stitch hem in place, sewing ¼ inch from edge all the way around.

To add a trim to the edge, measure the length and width of hemmed cloth. Add those measurements together and multiply by 2. Then divide by 36 to get yardage. The trims should be compatible with the fabric. For instance, a deep fringe would look great on a richly colored paisley but look tacky on a pastel gingham. If you're using a wide trim, reduce the measurement of your drop accordingly.

Sew trim to edge all the way around.

**

Quilted Tablerunner • Sewing

A tablerunner looks great by itself or atop a tablecloth as the setting for a centerpiece. A quilted tablerunner can take the place of potholders and trivets on the table or it can be used along a buffet for hot dishes at a potluck.

If used over a tablecloth, the runner should be the same length as the cloth. By itself, the runner should drop 6 inches on each end or be 24 inches shorter than the table (to allow for 12 inches at either end). The width could vary from 8-12 inches. The following directions are for a runner 10 inches wide and 5 feet long.

MATERIALS: Tissuc paper, paper bag, or newsprint for pattern; marker, pencil, or pen; scissors; straight pins; 1 yard 44/45-inch striped cotton fabric; crib-size quilt batting; 3⅔ yards flat eyelet trim, 1¼-inch wide; thread. (Yardages will differ for longer or shorter tablerunners. To determine yardage, figure desired length in inches and add 1 inch for seam allowance. Divide total by 2; then divide by 36 for yardage.)

DIRECTIONS: Enlarge pattern onto paper with heavy marker, pen, or pencil. Cut out 2 pattern pieces. Pre-wash fabric and press. Fold fabric in half lengthwise with selvages together. Pin pattern pieces, side-by-side, on fabric with length of pattern following the length of fabric. Cut out. You should now have 4 pieces.

Pin pattern pieces to quilt batting, trimming away center seam allowance. Using a ½-inch seam and with right sides together, stitch 2 fabric pieces together at center. Trim seam allowance and press flat. Repeat with other 2 fabric pieces. Pin quilt batting to wrong side of 1 seamed piece; baste close to all edges. Pin wrong side of other fabric piece to other side of batting, forming a fabric "sandwich" with batting in the middle. Sew layers together on all raw edges, stitching ¼ inch from all edges. Using a small, close stitch, zigzag between stitching and all raw edges.

Following stripes on one side of the runner, machine quilt runner. This will be the top of runner. Starting at center seam, pin eyelet trim to top of runner, placing evenly over the straight row of stitching. Pin all the way around runner, folding or mitering at the corners. At end, overlap trim, folding end of trim under. Sew trim to runner. Slip stitch trim together at ends.

VARIATIONS: Using this basic pattern, you can make several different types of runners. Some could be quilted or pieced together. Others could be left unquilted or with a square end. The trim could be varied for an entirely different look.

Following the same directions, you could make a large potholder or a placemat that could double as a foil to a centerpiece or a potholder for a large casserole dish. A third yard of fabric will make 2 potholders. You also will need a scrap of batting and 2½ yards of trim. The placemat requires ½ yard of fabric, a 12-by-18 inch piece of batting, and about 1½ yards of trim.

PATTERN FOR QUILTED TABLERUNNER

(1 square = 1 inch)

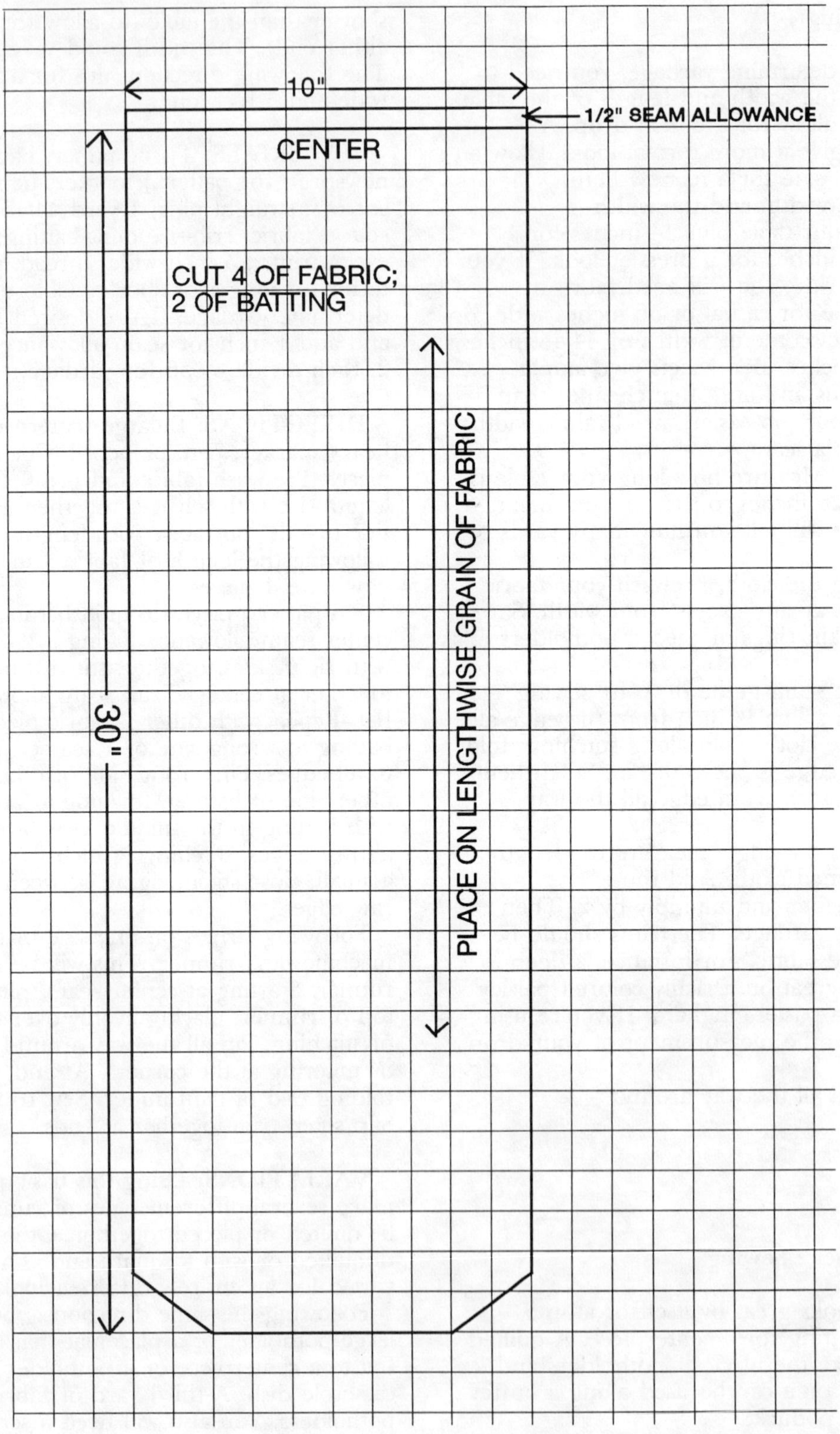

PATTERNS FOR QUILTED POTHOLDER AND PLACEMAT

(1 square = 1 inch)

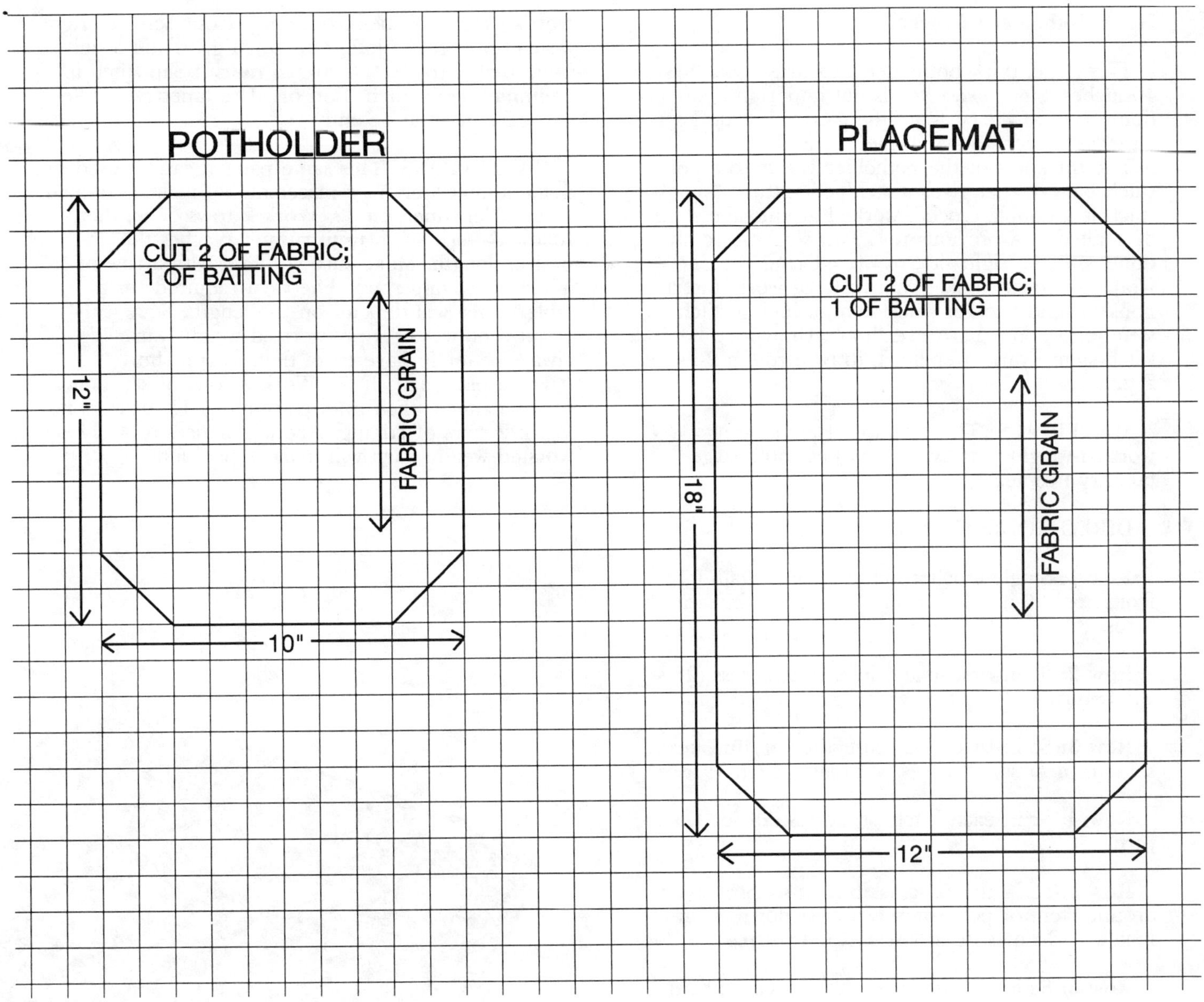

***

Hefty Potholder • Crochet

This large, thick potholder measures about 8½ by 10 inches. Since exact size is not important, you don't have to worry about the gauge. But do keep an even tension to avoid uneven results.

The thickness of the potholder is due to a post stitch pattern that gives it a ridged texture. A post stitch is a double crochet worked around the stem of a stitch in a previous row. Post stitches are always done with the right side of work facing you. To do, wrap yarn over hook. From front of work, insert hook around back of stitch stem, bringing stitch stem onto hook. Yarn over hook. Draw loop behind stitch stem, (yarn over hook, draw through 2 loops) 2 times.

MATERIALS: Three ounces 4-ply knitting worsted-weight yarn, size J crochet hook, large tapestry needle.

DIRECTIONS: Chain 28.

Row 1: Single crochet (sc) in second chain (ch) from hook. (First 2 ch count as 1 sc.) Sc in each ch across (28 sc). Ch 1; turn.

Row 2: Sc in first sc and in each sc across (28 sc). Ch 1; turn.

Row 3: Sc in first 2 sc, (post stitch around next sc, sc in next sc) 12 times, sc in last sc. Ch 1; turn.

Row 4: Sc in each stitch (st) across (28 sc). Ch 1; turn.

Row 5: Sc in first 2 sc, (skip next sc, post stitch around stem of post stitch two rows down, sc in next sc) 12 times, sc in last sc. Ch 1; turn.

Row 6: Sc in each st across (28 sc). Ch 1; turn.

Repeat rows 5 and 6 until potholder measures about 10 inches. End with a Row 6, including the ch 1; turn.

Edging, Row 1: Sc in each sc across top of potholder (28 sc), work 2 more sc in corner sc. Working down side, sc at end of each row, 3 sc in corner st. Sc across foundation ch, working 3 sc in corner st. Work 1 sc in end of each row up the remaining side. Work 2 more sc in beginning corner st; slip stitch in top of first sc. Ch 1; do not turn.

Row 2: Crab stitch in each sc all the way around. (A crab stitch is a sc worked backwards. In other words, you will be crocheting from left to right instead of right to left. This stitch gives you a tight, bound edge that won't stretch much.) Slip stitch in beginning crab stitch. End off. Use tapestry needle to weave in all loose ends.

VARIATIONS: This same pattern can be used to make a tablerunner or placemat. To make a 10-inch wide tablerunner, ch 32. Work 2 rows of sc; then follow pattern stitch until runner reaches the desired length. Make sure you end with a row of sc. Then do edging rows. The yarn required for a tablerunner will depend on the length. Start with about 9 ounces of 4-ply worsted weight yarn. It's always better to have extra than to run short.

For a placemat, ch 60. Work 2 rows of sc; then follow pattern stitch until placemat is 11 inches long. Work 2 rows of edging. About 9 ounces of 4-ply worsted weight yarn will make 1 placemat.

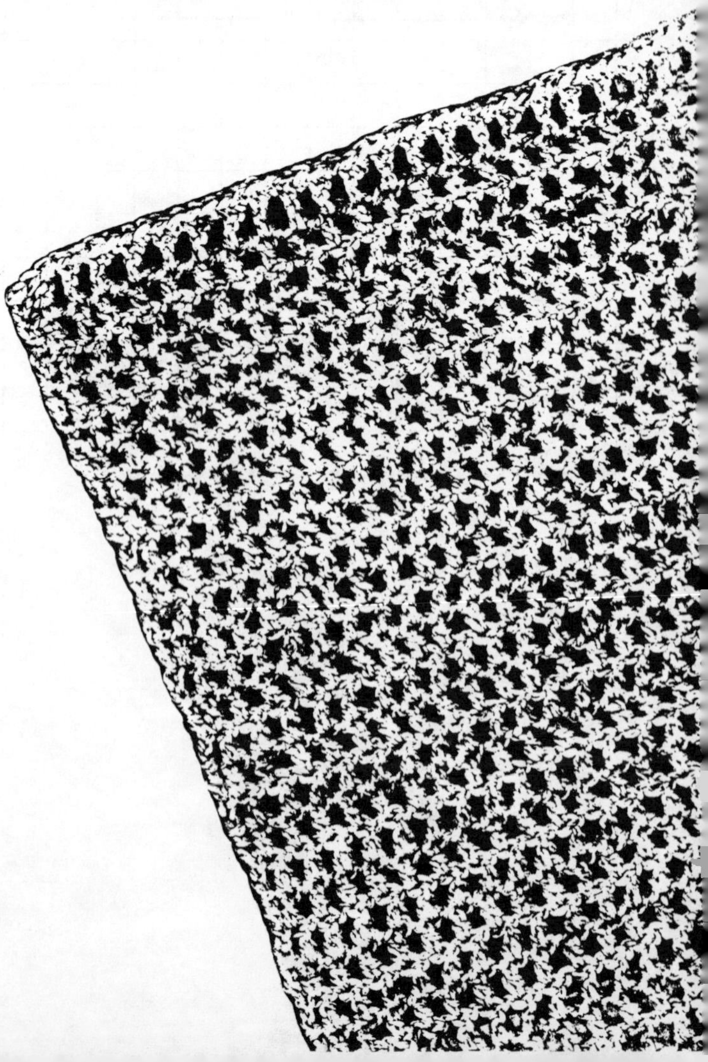

*

Cloth Napkins • Sewing

Cloth napkins are not a usual church accessory, but they go a long way toward dressing up a banquet. White napkins can also be used at Communion time or for baptisms.

Basic napkins are quite easy to make. More experienced crafters can dress them up with hand-crocheted edgings, lacy appliqués, embroidery, or open cutwork.

MATERIALS: One yard of a cotton/polyester fabric will make 4 napkins. Thread.

DIRECTIONS: Cut four 18-inch squares from fabric. Stitch ¼ inch from all raw edges on each napkin. Fold corners in diagonally along stitching. Fold sides at stitching line and then once more so raw edge is encased in a narrow hem. Pin. Stitch close to edge.

VARIATION: Instead of using a narrow hem, use a coordinating double-fold seam tape. Encase raw edges of napkin in seam tape and sew close to seam tape edge all the way around. You would need about 8 yards of seam tape to make 4 napkins.

**

Napkin Rings

If you're going to use cloth napkins, you need napkin rings. There are a lot of easy ways to make napkin rings. A carpenter could glue strips of molding together to form a square. The glued piece is then cut into 1-inch lengths, sanded, and stained or painted. Voilà, napkin rings.

Simpler napkin rings can be made by using 1-inch wide woven trims or ribbon. Cut into 5-inch lengths. Fold in half with right sides together. Stitch ½-inch seam. Trim seam allowance. Turn ring right side out.

Scraps of fabric left over from tablecloths can be braided together for a country-style napkin ring. Cut the scraps into ⅝-inch widths. Finish raw edges with a narrow zigzag stitch, pinking shears, or glue. Baste the ends of 3 strips together. Braid. Cut braid into 5-inch lengths, carefully securing all ends. Fold in half with right sides together. Stitch ½-inch seam. Trim seam allowance. Turn right side out.

Crocheted napkin rings also lend a country look. Use a size J hook and a scrap of coordinating yarn. Ch 15; join with a slip stitch to beginning ch.

Rnd 1: Ch 2 (counts as 1 sc), sc in each ch around (16 sc), join with a slip stitch in top of ch 2.

Rnd 2: Working in front loop only, ch 4 (counts as dc and ch), skip sc, (dc in next sc, skip sc, ch 1) 7 times, slip stitch in third ch of ch 4.

Rnd 3: Working in back loop only, ch 2 (counts as sc), sc in each ch and dc all the way around (16 sc), join with a slip stitch in top of ch 2. End off. Weave in loose ends.

DRESSING THE WINDOWS

One of the ugliest spots in a church sanctuary, unless it is blessed with stained glass, is the window. Some churches have tinted or textured window glass to keep worshipers from being distracted by something outside. But even these can look stark and cold.

Church windows can be dressed much the same as those of a home. Curtains or drapes in keeping with the atmosphere of the sanctuary give a cozy look to the room. Even a valance going solo can soften the harsh glare of a window.

At the least, a candle arrangement on each window sill will add some warmth. A log chapel in southeastern Idaho used votive candles in hobbled ruby glass holders to reflect their light against the plain windows at night. The dim candlelight flickered a glow of a bygone era over the room's seating—antique theater seats from the old Orpheum Theater in San Francisco.

At Christmas, the votives were replaced with tall tapers in simple brass candlesticks. A glass hurricane globe was placed over each candle. Pine cones and plaid bows were arranged around the bottom of the globes.

Wide window sills can also be dressed with baskets, simple pottery, even things from nature, such as shells, leaves, or a spray of dried flowers.

When you want a more completed look, go with curtains or drapes. For a country decor, lace panels or muslin curtains look fine. Heavy drapes, sheers, or even mini-blinds would look good in a more formal or modern setting.

While good drapes require the expertise of a professional seamstress, curtains for any room in the church can be made by the less experienced. An ambitious crocheter could take on the task of creating lace panels for the windows. For a straight, shade-type panel, measure the inside width and length of the window. Use a small suspension rod or wooden dowel to hang the panel on the inside of the window casing.

**

Hourglass Curtains • Sewing

A school teacher in a mountain chapel surprised her congregation one Sunday with new muslin curtains on each of the narrow bare windows in the sanctuary. The curtains were gathered on curtain rods at both the top and bottom and caught in the middle with a tieback. The whole project had taken some of the teacher's precious weekend time, but it was a gift appreciated by the whole congregation.

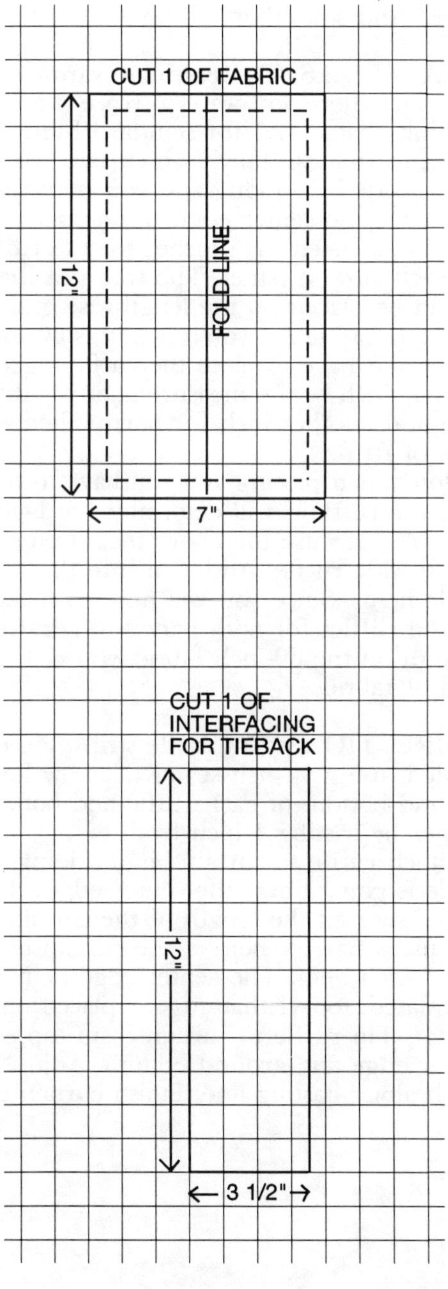

TIEBACK PATTERN FOR HOURGLASS CURTAIN

(1 square = 1 inch) — — — stitching line

MATERIALS: Measuring tape; heavy muslin (yardage will depend on size of window); thread; 2 small suspension rods for each window; scrap of interfacing; large snap or Velcro fastener.

DIRECTIONS: Measure inside width of window. Multiply measurement by 1.25; then add 2. This is the width measurement for your fabric. (For example, a 36-inch wide window would need fabric at least 47 inches wide to avoid extra seams.) Then, measure the inside length of window and add 4 inches for casings. Divide length total by 36 for yardage. (A window 45 inches long would need 1⅜ yards of fabric.)

Cut fabric according to measurements. Hem both sides, using a 1-inch hem. Turn under ½ inch at both top and bottom. Press. Turn under another 1½ inches at top and bottom for casing. Stitch 1¼ inch from edge. Put a suspension rod in each casing. Place in windows, easing fullness of curtain evenly.

Use a matching tieback to pull the curtain in at the middle. To make the tieback, cut a piece of fabric 12 inches long by 7 inches wide. Cut fusible interfacing 12 inches long by 3½ inches wide. Apply interfacing to wrong side of fabric, placing one long edge of interfacing at center fold line of fabric. Fold fabric in half, lengthwise, placing right sides together. Using a ½-inch seam, stitch edges together at both ends and side, leaving an opening for turning. Grade edges. Turn right side out. Press. Slip stitch opening. Top stitch ¼ inch from edge all the way around tieback. Center large snap or Velcro fastener at ends to hold tieback together.

*

Curtains • Sewing

Making curtains or tiers is a simple task as all seams are straight and there are not a lot of parts to assemble. Accurate measuring and even cutting are probably the most important part. A sagging hem, curved edge, or uneven top will mark a curtain as homemade no matter how much time and materials you put into the project.

MATERIALS: Measuring tape; sturdy, washable fabric; thread; 1-inch wide curtain rod.

DIRECTIONS: Most curtains fit on the outside of the window casing, with an inch margin on each side. Where you place the top of the curtain depends on your taste and whether you want to lengthen a short window or minimize a long one. Whatever you do, be consistent with all windows in the room.

Measure the width by starting an inch on the outside of one casing to an inch on the outside of the other casing. Multiply by 1.5 (for extra full curtains, multiply by 2). Add 4 inches for side hems. Divide the total by 2 to get width measurement for each curtain panel. (Going with the standard fullness of 150 percent, a 36-inch window would need two panels, each 29 inches wide. To avoid extra seams, you would need to get fabric 60 inches wide.)

Measure the length you want the curtain to be from top to bottom. Add 7 inches for hem and casing. Divide total by 36 for yardage—if the fabric is wide enough for 2 panels.

Fold fabric in half, lengthwise. Using measurements, mark and cut curtain panels. Press under ½ inch on bottom of each panel. Fold under 3 inches for hem. Blind or hem stitch in place.

Press under ¼ inch on each side of both panels. Fold under ¾ inch for hem. Stitch in place.

Press under ½ inch at top of each panel. Fold under 3 inches for casing. Stitch close to bottom of casing. Stitch second row 1¼ inches from top. Place on curtain rod; adjust fullness and hang.

**

Ruffles • Sewing

Ruffles can dress up plain curtains or add country charm to a valance or tieback. They can be made from matching or coordinating fabric such as eyelet, calico, lace, or gingham.

There are as many different ways of making ruffles as there are types of curtains and valances. They can range from a few inches wide to 10 inches or so. Some are attached with a seam, while others have headers and are sewn onto the top of the curtain.

First, decide how deep a ruffle you want and where you want the ruffle. Some curtain ruffles are just along the bottom. Others run down the center edges. And still others do both.

MATERIALS: To determine yardage, measure the edge where you want to place the ruffle. Multiply that by 1.5 for standard fullness or by 2 for extra fullness. (Say each curtain panel is 29 inches wide by 36 long and you want the ruffle to run down the center edge and across the bottom. You would need 97½ inches for the ruffle length for each curtain panel. The width of the ruffle should be placed on the lengthwise grain of the fabric. If the fabric you're using is 60 inches wide, you would have to piece the ruffle together so add another inch to the measurement for that seam, then add another inch for narrow hems at both ends of ruffle.)

How much piecing you will have to do and how wide the ruffle is will determine yardage. For example, let's use the above measurements with a 6-inch wide ruffle. Add 1 inch to the width for the ruffle hems. Since you will need to make four strips for the ruffles for both panels to get them long enough on the 60-inch fabric, you will need ⅞ of a yard of fabric.

DIRECTIONS: Cut ruffle strips. Piece together as needed, using ½-inch seams. Narrow hem both the top and bottom of each ruffle and both ends. Gather by basting 1 inch from top.

Attach ruffle to curtain before doing casing if the ruffle is going down the center edges. If using a ruffle, shorten the length of the curtain accordingly and use a narrow hem at the curtain bottom instead of a 3-inch hem. The center edge hem can be eliminated, too, if that edge is placed on the fabric selvage. Pin ruffle to curtain from top edge along center edge and around bottom. Adjust gathers. Stitch along basting line. Finish curtain casing.

**

Tiebacks

A switch in tiebacks can give a fresh look to your drapes and curtains. Some churches have a variety of tiebacks in colors for each liturgical season. Such tiebacks can be plain, embroidered, appliqued, or hand-painted.

CROCHETED CHECKERBOARD: Use a cotton crochet thread in a color to complement your drapes or curtains and a size 1 steel crochet hook. Chain (ch) 30.

Row 1: Double crochet (dc) in 4th ch from hook. (First 3 ch count as 1 dc.) Dc in next ch; (ch 2, skip 2 ch, dc in each of next 3 ch) 5 times. Ch 3; turn.

Row 2: Ch 2; skip 2 dc; dc twice in ch space; (ch 3, skip 3 dc, dc twice in ch space) 4 times; ch 2; skip 2 dc; dc in top of ch 3. Ch 3; turn.

Row 3: Two dc in ch space; ch 2; skip 2 dc; (3 dc in ch space, ch 2, skip 2 dc) 4 times; 2 dc in ch space; dc in top of ch 3. Ch 3; turn.

Repeat Rows 2 and 3 until tieback reaches desired length. After last row, ch 1 instead of 3. Work 1 row of single crochet all the way around tieback, working 3 single crochet in each corner. At end, join with a slip stitch to first single crochet. End off. Weave in loose ends. Attach rings or thread loops at each end to go over hooks in wall.

CROCHETED SHELL: Use cotton crochet thread and size 1 steel crochet hook. Ch 32.

Row 1: 5 dc in 5th ch from hook (first 3 ch count as 1 dc); skip 1 ch; 1 dc in next ch; (skip 1 ch, 5 dc in next ch, skip 1 ch, 1 dc in next ch) 6 times; ch 3; turn.

Row 2: Skip 2 dc; 5 dc in third dc of shell; skip 2 dc; dc in next dc; (skip 2 dc, 5 dc in third dc of shell, skip 2 dc, dc in next dc) 6 times. Ch 3; turn.

Repeat Row 2 until tieback measures desired length. At end of last row, do not ch 3. End off. Weave in loose ends. Attach rings or thread loops at each end to go over hooks on wall.

GATHERED ROPE TIEBACK: These heavy tiebacks look best with drapes. They should be made from a heavy, nubby fabric such as a linen or antique satin. You will need a piece of fabric 3¼ inches wide by 49½ inches long. You also will need a piece of cording or rope about ¾ inch in diameter and 33 inches long.

With right sides together, fold fabric in half lengthwise. Using a ⅝-inch seam, stitch side seam, leaving both ends open. Trim seam; press seam allowance open. Turn right side out.

Hook a large safety pin to one end of rope. Thread rope through fabric tube, pushing fabric into even gathers around rope. Temporarily secure rope ends about ⅝ inch from each end of fabric. Turn in fabric seam allowance at both ends; slip stitch, catching in rope ends securely. Attach rings or thread loops at each end to go over wall hooks.

PUCKERED TIEBACK: This kind of tieback looks better on a lightweight curtain or drape. Use a sheer fabric such as polyester voile. You will need a strip of fabric 9¼ inches wide by 51 inches long.

French seam long edges together. To do a French seam, fold fabric in half, lengthwise, with WRONG sides together. Stitch a ⅜-inch seam. Trim close to stitching. Turn inside out. Stitch ¼ inch from previous stitching, encasing raw edges. Using a ⅝-inch seam, stitch both ends, leaving an opening in one end for turning. Turn; press. Slip stitch opening.

Baste down center of tieback (2 inches from either edge). Adjust gathers so tieback measures 33 inches. Stitch over basting. Attach rings or thread loops at both ends to go over wall hooks.

A ruffle can also be used as a tieback. Or sew a ruffle to a 1-inch wide tieback. A plain tieback could be dressed up with fringe, trim, lace, or eyelet. A sash-type tieback could be adorned with a big country bow complete with long streamers.

Other ideas for tiebacks include using a wide grosgrain ribbon, braided fabric, long strips of needlepoint, macrame, or silk cords knotted and fringed at the ends.

Valances

Valances, by themselves or over drapes or curtains, change the look of a window. They can be ballooned, pleated, ruffled, gathered, draped, or straight in matching or coordinating fabrics. Pattern books abound with patterns for various valances. Simpler looks can be achieved by merely draping long pieces of cloth or crocheted or knitted lace over a curtain rod. The cloth can be twisted, swooped, or stretched taut. Just experiment to get the look you want, anchoring the valance behind the curtain rods at the corners.

If you use a 36-inch or 45-inch fabric, all you will need to do is narrow hem the piece at both ends. The length of the piece will depend on how much drape or swoop you want. Try twisting two lengths of coordinating fabric together for a different look.

An alternative to a valance is a wooden or padded cornice. Anyone skilled with a jigsaw or circular saw could turn plywood into decorative cornices that could be stained, painted, stenciled, or covered with fabric.

Another valance alternative would be to put a wooden shelf right above the window. Decorate with miniature churches, baskets, bouquets, candlesticks, antique Bibles, praying hands—whatever is available.

SETTING THE MOOD FOR WORSHIP

Much has been written in recent years about the significance of worship in church life. And there has been an emphasis on pulling today's churches out of the worship doldrums. Worship seminars are held across the country. Teachers, seminary professors, and denominational executives urge pastors and students to help meet the soul hunger for dynamic worship. Professional journals dedicate entire issues to this one aspect of Christian life.

Stodgy worship patterns are changing as a new awareness that we gather to celebrate a living God of resurrection permeates our churches.

True worship originates deep within a person's own spirit. Worship that is pleasing and acceptable to God must flow from the heart. But pleasant surroundings, flowers, greenery, and other items of beauty will do much to help worshipers center their thoughts on God, the Creator.

Altar or Communion tables can be draped with remnants of beautiful fabrics, set with a simple vase of flowers or an elaborate floral arrangement, adorned with candles and an open Bible, decorated with a basketful of silk flowers, covered with autumn leaves or branches of spring blossoms.

Altar cloths and matching pulpit stoles can be made from small pieces of rich fabrics appliqued or embroidered with crosses, or crocheted or knitted for a different look. Fortunate is the church that has an assortment of altar and pulpit coverings for use during the various liturgical seasons.

When decorating the front of the sanctuary, don't overlook the piano and organ if they are in plain view. Make runners to match the altar cloths for the top of the instruments; set coordinating flowers or candles on them for continuity.

***

Organ Bench Pad • Crochet

A soft organ or piano bench cover will be appreciated by the accompanist. And it is small details like this that give your sanctuary a warm, cared-for look.

MATERIALS: 1 large ball white or natural cotton crochet thread; size 1 steel crochet hook; ⅞ yard heavy fabric such as waleless corduroy, upholstery velvet, or antique satin; 14-inch by 29-inch piece of quilt batting; thread.

DIRECTIONS: With crochet thread, chain (ch) 83 (should measure 13 inches long).

Row 1: 5 double crochet (dc) in fifth ch from hook (first 3 ch count as 1 dc); skip 1 ch; dc in next ch; (skip 1 ch, 5 dc in next ch, skip 1 ch, dc in next ch) all the way to end. Ch 3; turn.

Row 2: Skip 2 dc; 5 dc in third dc of shell; skip 2 dc; dc in next dc; (skip 2 dc, 5 dc in third dc of shell, skip 2 dc, dc in next dc) all the way to end. Ch 3; turn.

Repeat Row 2 until piece is 28 inches long. At end of last row, end off instead of ch 3. Weave in loose ends.

Make pattern by cutting a 14-inch by 29-inch rectangle. Fold fabric in half, lengthwise. Pin pattern in place; cut. Cut 1 pattern piece from quilt batting. Pin batting to wrong side of 1 fabric piece; baste close to all edges. Place crocheted piece on right side of fabric, allowing a ½-inch fabric seam allowance on all sides of the crocheting. Sew crocheting in place. Pin fabric pieces right sides together. Stitch ½-inch seam around all edges, leaving an opening for turning. Turn; slip stitch opening.

Using the same pattern, you could make quilted, appliquéd, embroidered, or cross-stitched bench pads.

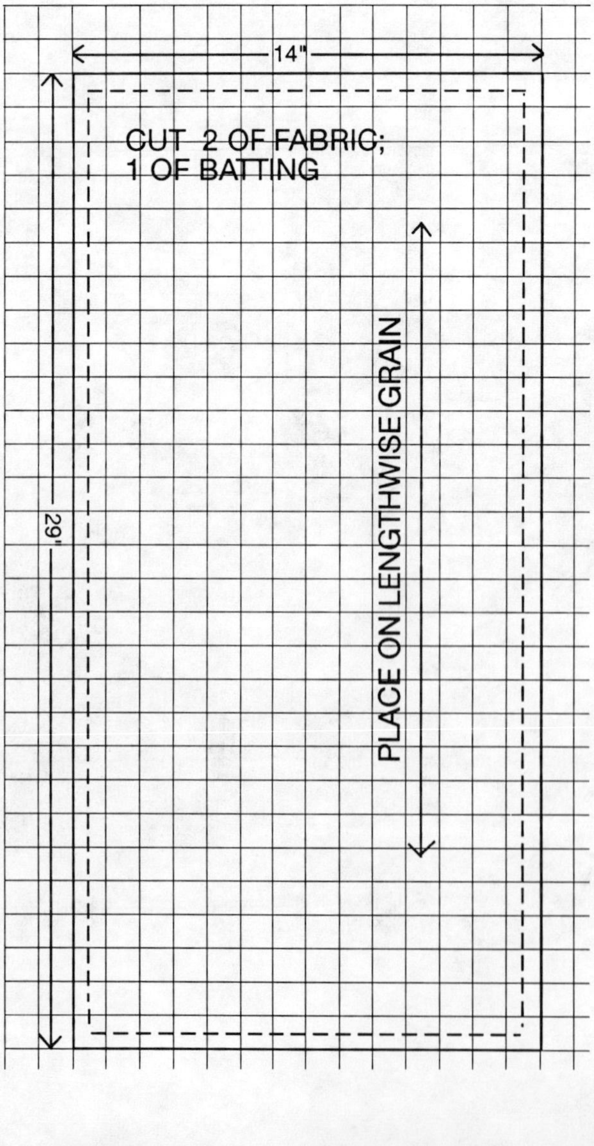

PATTERN FOR ORGAN BENCH PAD

(1 square = 1 inch) — — — sewing line

*

Rugged Cross • Craft

Seasonal decorating is done in most churches for Advent and Easter, but many congregations leave their sanctuaries bare the rest of the year. It doesn't have to be that way.

For instance, when the Christmas holidays are over, instead of removing the Christmas tree, strip its limbs, leaving only the "cross" branches. Stand the "rugged cross" in a conspicuous spot. On Ash Wednesday, drape it in black and leave it through Lent. Around Good Friday, you may want to fashion a crown of thorns and hang it over the cross.

On Easter, drape the cross in vibrant purple and set Easter lillies at its base.

If your church has a large cross hanging in the front or in some other prominent place, it could be draped in the same manner from Christmas through Easter.

Using an opaque projector (available at rental stores) and a picture of a lamb, make a large poster board lamb. Project the picture onto the white poster board and draw around it. With markers, draw on the features, then cut the lamb out with a sharp knife. Place the lamb at the foot of the cross with a large, neatly lettered sign: "Behold the Lamb of God. . . ."

The same method can be used to produce large cardboard animals for a nativity scene.

*

Greenery • Flowers

Christmas floral arrangements are perhaps the simplest of all altar decorations, as so much can be done with pine cones and greens. Use a large, oblong block of florist foam (white foam packing works well, too) and stick evergreen branches around it till the foundation is pleasing to the eye. With a hot glue gun, attach several large pine cones to the arrangement and a large bow.

For variety, cut small holes in the block and insert a couple of tall red candles. Or cut a slit in the foam block and insert a holiday pewter plate in it. Arrange greens around the plate, a couple of candles off to one side, and perhaps a red carnation or two kept fresh by wrapping the stems in soaked paper or inserted in a small flower water container.

In place of the plate, you could insert a wooden craft goose, lamb, or duck. Tie a holiday bow around its neck.

*

Advent Wreaths • Craft

Advent wreaths are easy to make and limited only by your imagination. Using a grapevine wreath, insert four candles at intervals around the circle. In the middle, place a large, fat, white candle. Each Sunday of Advent, light one more candle. At your Christmas service, light all four, plus the center one, signifying that "the Light of the World" has come.

Green wreaths can also be used as the base of the Advent wreath or use an extra-large candle ring.

Candles could be placed in cored apples circling a tall taper for a unique Advent setting. Or use brass candlesticks arranged in a circle around a taller candlestick.

**

Altar Cloth • Crochet

Altar cloths can be pieces cut from fabric, narrow hemmed all the way around, and draped over the altar. They can be appliqued with crosses or edged with rich fringe. Or they can be simple cloths of homespun. Lace runners also add charm to the altar table, or stretched across the top of a piano or organ.

This cloth uses 4-ply worsted weight yarn to work up quickly for the winter months. It looks best when worked in white or in a light neutral shade.

SIZE: About 1 foot by 3 feet.

MATERIALS: 4 ounces yarn; size D crochet hook; large tapestry needle.

GAUGE: 9 double crochet = 2 inches; 5 rows = 2 inches.

DIRECTIONS: Loosely ch 166. (Ch 3 counts as 1 dc.)

Row 1: Dc in 4th ch from hook and in each remaining ch across (164 dc, counting ch 3). Ch 3; turn.

Row 2: Dc in each of next 3 dc; (ch 4, skip 4 dc, dc in each of next 4 dc) all the way across. Ch 3; turn.

Row 3: (Dc in each of next 2 dc, ch 5, skip 1 dc and 4 ch, dc in each of next 4 dc, ch 5, skip 4 ch and 1 dc) all the way across; dc in each of last 3 dc. Ch 3; turn.

Row 4: (Dc in each of next 2 dc, ch 5, skip 5 ch, dc in each of next 4 dc, ch 5, skip 5 ch) all the way across; dc in each of last 3 dc. Ch 3; turn.

Row 5: (Dc in each of next 2 dc, ch 3, skip 3 ch, dc in each of next 2 ch, dc in each of next 4 dc, dc in each of next 2 ch, ch 3, skip 3 ch) all the way across; dc in each of last 3 dc. Ch 3; turn.

Row 6: (Dc in each of next 2 dc, ch 3, skip 3 ch, dc in each of next 8 dc, ch 3, skip 3 ch) all the way across; dc in each of last 3 dc. Ch 3; turn.

Row 7: (Dc in each of next 2 dc, ch 5, skip 3 ch and 2 dc, dc in each of next 4 dc, ch 5, skip 2 dc and 3 ch) all the way across; dc in each of last 3 dc. Ch 3; turn.

Row 8: (Dc in each of next 2 dc, dc in next ch, ch 4, skip 4 ch, dc in each of next 4 dc, ch 4, skip 4 ch, dc in next ch) all the way across; dc in each of last 3 dc. Ch 3; turn.

Row 9: Dc in next dc and in each dc and ch across (164 dc). Ch 3; turn.

Row 10: Dc in next dc and in each dc across.

Rows 11-22: Repeat Row 10 twelve times.

Row 23: Repeat Row 2.

Row 24: Repeat Row 3.

Row 25: Repeat Row 5.

Row 26: Repeat Row 6.

Row 27: Repeat Row 7.

Row 28: Repeat Row 4.

Row 29: Repeat Row 8.

Row 30: Repeat Row 9. Instead of ch 3 at end, ch 1. Do not turn.

Edging: Single crochet evenly around all sides of runner. End off. Weave in loose ends with tapestry needle.

*

Stenciled Rugs • Art

Often overlooked is the floor. But even your rugs can welcome people to your church and let them know they are in the house of the Lord.

A quick way to make rugs for the church is with carpet remnants or runners. Using fabric paints and stencils, you can create unique rugs. Or you can use masking tape to create stripes or other geometric shapes. Quilt templates or cookie cutters could also be used for pattern ideas or to create a checkerboard effect. The designs can form a border around the rug, provide an all-over pattern, or form a central focus point on the rug. Praying hands, crosses, or other symbols could be painted onto the carpet pieces.

DIRECTIONS: Plan your design. Work with one color paint at a time. Mask off what you don't want painted with that color. Using a suitably sized paintbrush, daub the paint onto the carpet, twirling the brush so the paint gets to the stems of the carpet loops. Let dry. As soon as the paint dries, "comb" that spot with an old fork to lift the nap. Continue with the next color.

CREATING QUILTS

For generations, the old-time quilting bee was one of the social events for women in many rural churches. They'd get together to craft quilts for newlyweds, new arrivals, and families hit by disaster. It was a time of fellowship, showing off needlework, and, yes, catching up on the latest gossip. As the church's grasp on community life weakened, the church quilting bee faded away.

But, today, as quilting enjoys a resurgence, the quilting frames, needles, and thimbles are finding their way back into church fellowship halls. And once again, Christians are experiencing the camaraderie that is born of working together on a project from the heart,

With all the advances in the art of quilting, it is not as formidable a task as our grandmothers faced. Templates, rotary cutters, cutting mats, pre-sized bats, adjustable frames, and sewing machines all make the job much simpler. And for the completely uninitiated, there's a wide array of fabrics in patchwork prints. One has only to add the batting and backing and then stitch or tie around the designs already printed on the fabric.

For the beginner, baby quilts are among the easiest. In some churches, quilters make a baby quilt for the first baby born into each family in the congregation. This practice can cause some hard feelings if the guidelines aren't established first. Someone may get hurt feelings if a quilt isn't made for a new grandchild whose parents grew up in the church but now live 100 miles away. Sometimes it works better if some of the quilters make the quilt on their own and give it as a shower gift instead of establishing a church tradition that can get out of hand.

If you are new to quilting, start with the church nursery. Nice baby quilts always come in handy in the nursery.

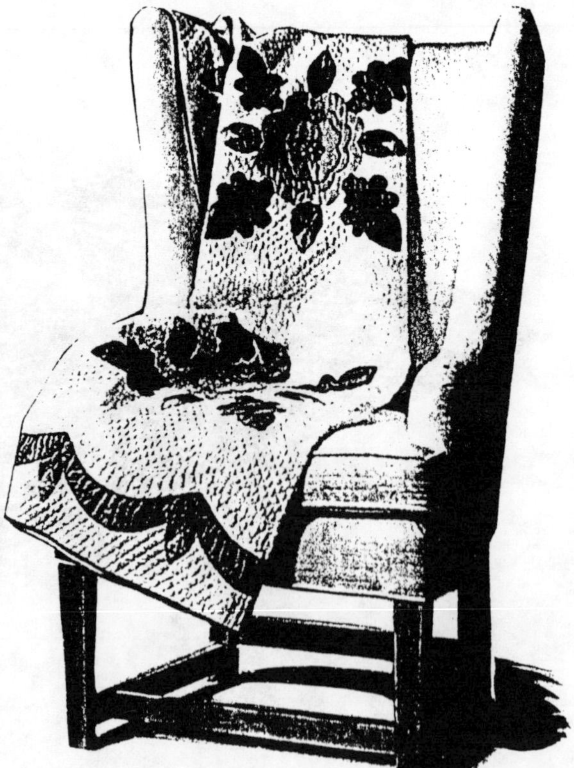

*

Tufted Baby Quilt • Quilting

Most fabric stores have a selection of preprinted quilt patterns especially for babies. These make assembling a lovely baby quilt much simpler and quicker.

MATERIALS: A fabric panel; ruffled eyelet trim (about 5 inches longer than the combined measurements of all four sides of panel); soft flannel in a coordinating fabric (should be the same size as the panel on all sides); crib-size polyester quilt batting (cotton isn't as washable and will lump); coordinating baby yarn; embroidery needle with large eye.

DIRECTIONS: Preshrink fabric. Cut panel to size, allowing for a ⅝-inch seam allowance around all sides. With right sides together, pin eyelet trim just inside seam allowance, mitering at corners and seaming trim where the two ends meet. Stitch.

Using tailor tacks or a light pencil, mark evenly spaced points on the top for the ties. For a baby quilt, ties should be 3 or 4 inches apart.

Place flannel lining, wrong side up, on work surface. Place batting on top of lining. Smooth out any wrinkles. Baste batting to lining. Baste o… from edge and down the center of both length… width.

Turn lining over so flannel faces up. Place quilt top, wrong side up, on top of lining. Pin around edges. Stitch a ⅝-inch seam around edges, leaving a large opening for turning at one end. Grade seams. Turn. Press in seam allowance of opening; slip stitch opening.

Thread embroidery needle with yarn. Using a double strand of yarn, follow the tufting pattern on quilt top. Work from the center out. For each tie, push needle from top to lining, leaving about 5 inches of yarn on top. Push needle back up to surface, about ¼ inch away. For a secure tie, push needle back down to lining and up again one more time. Tie yarn in a firm double knot. Clip ends to desired length. Repeat over entire quilt.

VARIATIONS: Similar quilts can be made without the eyelet ruffle. Instead of using baby yarn for the tufts, use candlewick yarn, cotton crochet thread, or several strands of embroidery floss. For a plainer quilt, use 1⅔ yards of any fabric for the top and 1⅔ yards of a coordinating fabric for the lining. A finished crib quilt should measure 40 by 60 inches.

MAKING YARN TUFTS

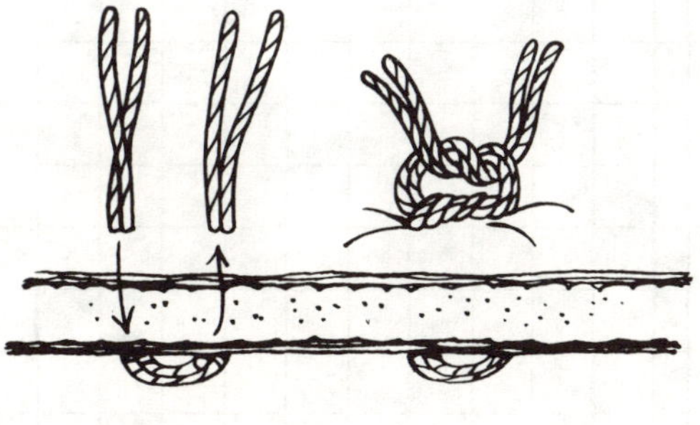

NG DIAGRAM FOR BABY QUILT

square = 2 inches) — — basting line

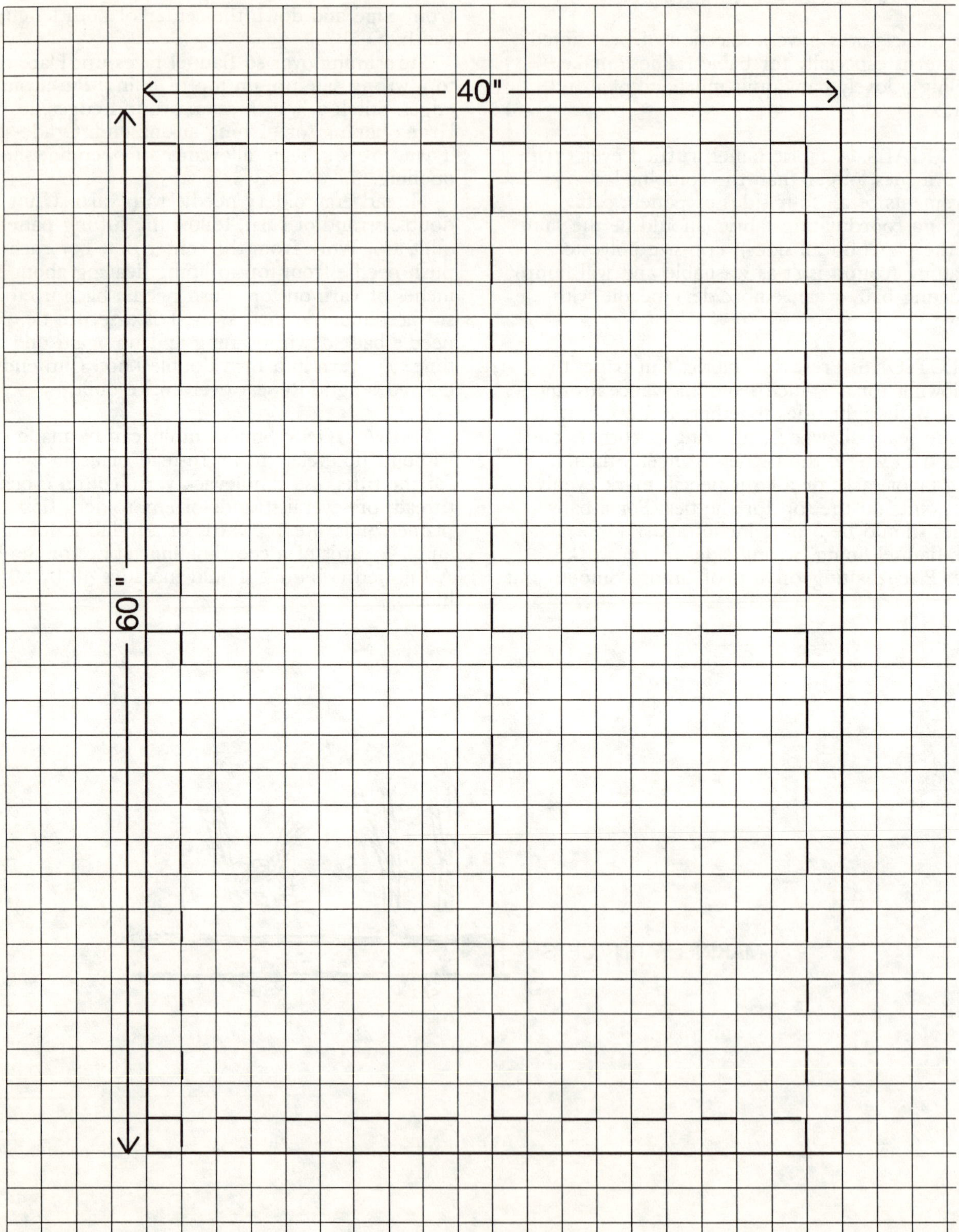

PLAYMAT PATTERN: HOUSE

(1 square = 2 inches)

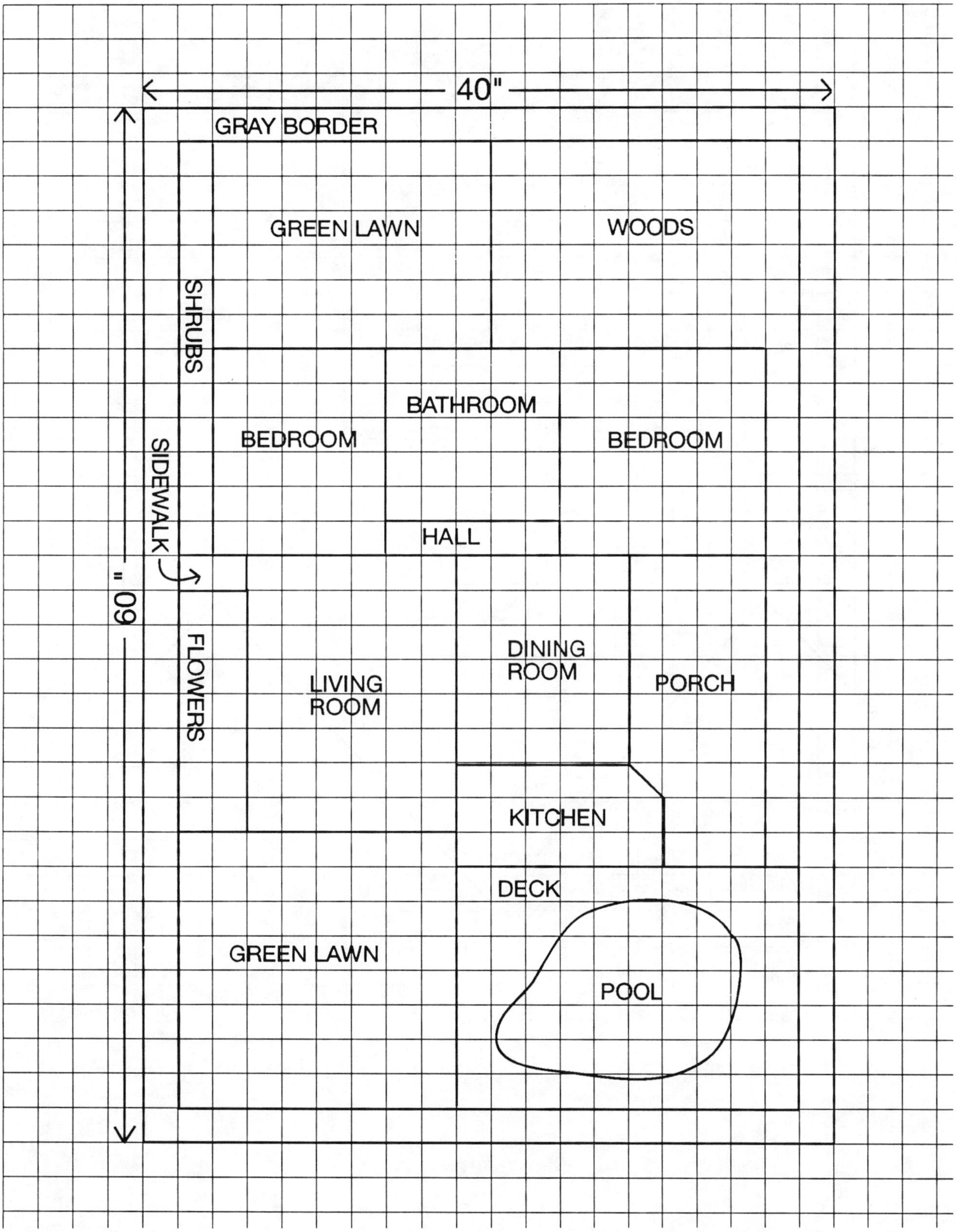

BORDER DIAGRAM FOR PLAYMAT

(drawn to size)

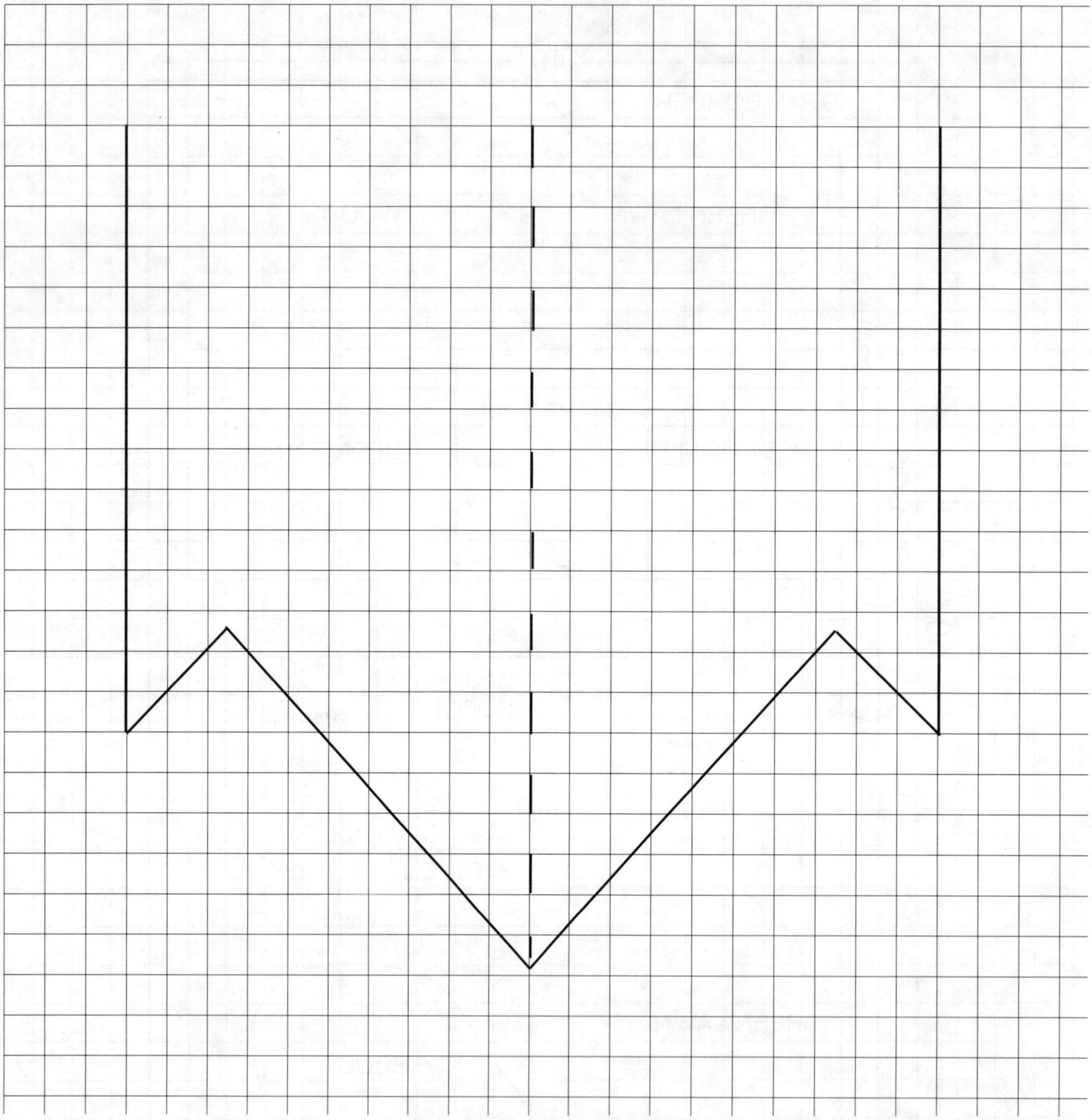

PLAYMAT PATTERN: FIELDS

(1 square = 2 inches)

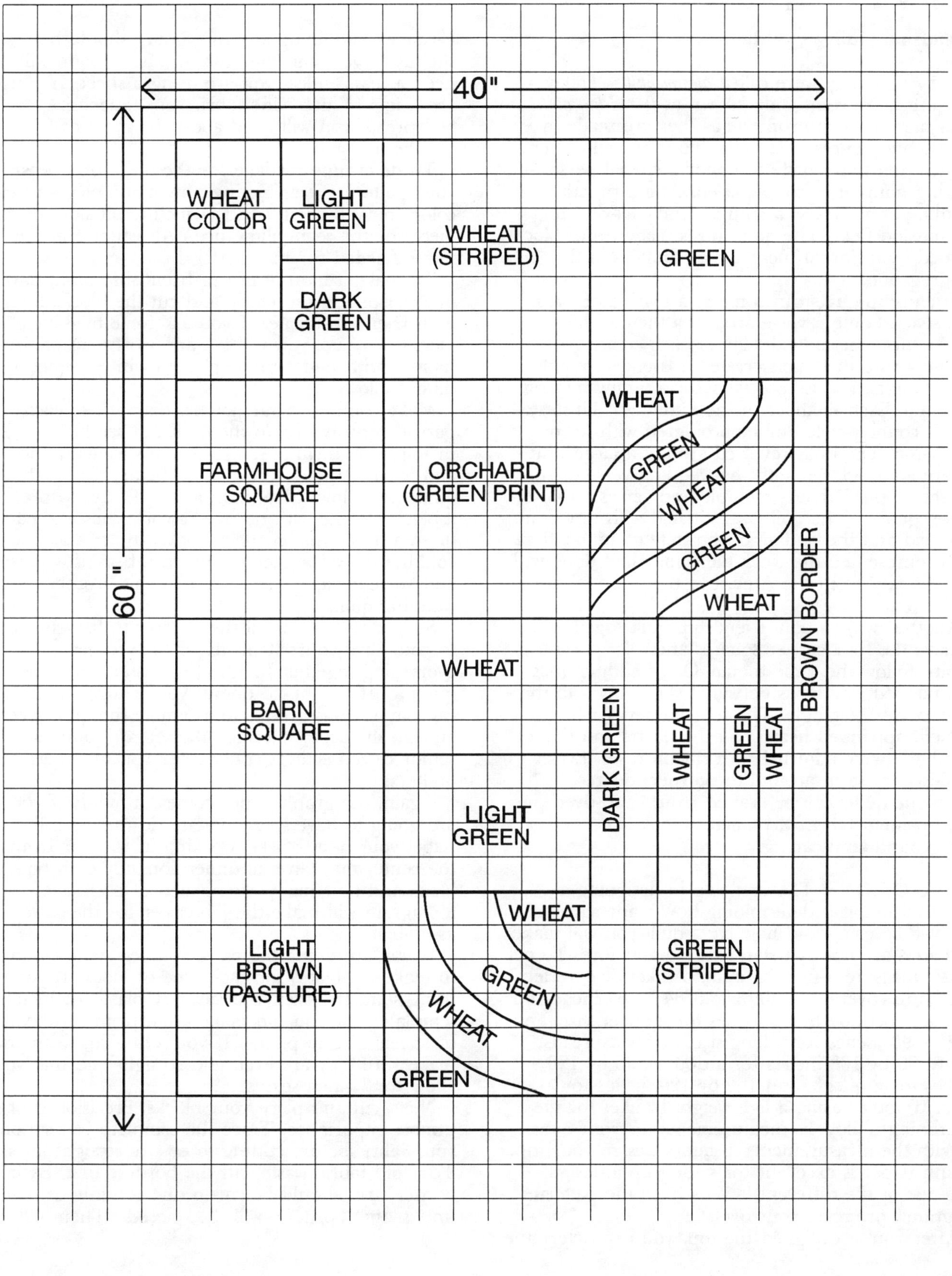

**

Friendship Quilt • Quilting

Long ago, they were called *album quilts*. Today, they are more commonly known as *friendship quilts*. Both names are appropriate as they are made by friends and represent a quilt album of well-wishers.

Such quilts are made to honor a special person—a retiring minister, a couple celebrating a fiftieth wedding anniversary, a church family leaving for the mission field. The quilt top is made up of blocks created by different members or families in the congregation.

Friendship quilts can come in a myriad of sizes and styles. Some revolve around a theme while others show the individuality of each creator.

One group in Illinois created a friendship quilt from blue and white polyester for a family moving to Idaho. Each member of the family was illustrated with a country-style doll embroidered with his or her name. The dolls revolved around a large white square embroidered with the wedding verse of the parents. Other friends embroidered verses on other white squares. The quilt was stitched with tiny Stars of David and the outline of the state of Idaho. The stars represented the work the family had done with a missionary from the American Board of Missions to the Jews.

Another way to tie a friendship quilt together is to have the four corner squares and a large central square follow the same theme. One wedding quilt had padded love birds entwined with ribbon in the large center rectangle. The four corners each had stuffed, appliqued hearts. All the hearts and the love birds were adorned with ribbon roses. Eyelet ruffles were sewn around the corner squares.

Unique quilts can be crafted from hand-dyed or hand-painted fabrics arranged to look like background landscaping.

DIRECTIONS: The first step in designing a friendship quilt is determining how many squares you will be using and how big a quilt you will make. Bed sizes are not that standardized anymore. To get a size, measure a favorite quilt, blanket or coverlet. Or figure coverlet sizes at about 84 by 84 inches for a double bed, 94 by 90 inches for a queen size, and 112 by 90 inches for a king size. For bedspreads, figure 90 by 108 inches for a double, 96 by 120 inches for a queen, and 120 by 120 inches for a king. If you're using a lightweight blanket for the interlining, follow its measurements for your quilt.

With the measurements in mind, design your top. Graph paper is excellent for setting up a design. Use one of the different layouts from the pattern diagrams, or create your own.

After you've designed the top, you can determine yardage. The lining and interlining should be slightly larger than the quilt top. The lining will need a seam unless you are using a sheet. If you are using 45-inch wide fabric for a queensize bedspread, you will need about 10 yards of fabric for the lining.

To determine yardage for the quilt top, measure your pattern pieces, noting how many pieces of each color you will need. (Add ¼ inch to all sides of each piece for the seam allowance.) Also figure in the fabric needed for the borders.

To make a more uniform friendship quilt, have one person get the fabric and cut the blocks for each friend to create. If you ask for 8-by-8-inch blocks of white, you will get an assortment of sizes, fabrics, and shades ranging from whitest white to dingy yellow.

Make copies of your pattern diagram so each person contributing to the quilt can see how it will fit together. Include scraps of the various fabrics and let the friends know what theme, if any, the quilt will follow. Give them ideas of ways to prepare a block. People with no needlework skills can paint or stencil designs on their block. An art major who couldn't thread a needle painted a beautiful sunset and verse on a square he did for his brother's wedding quilt.

Set a deadline for all the squares to be returned to you. Give yourself plenty of time to get everything together for the final assembling and quilting. If you or no one in your church quilts, you can pay various groups to assemble the quilt pieces and do the actual piecing. Many craft boutiques or senior citizen centers could refer you to expert quilters.

Again, the graph paper comes in handy if you are going to have someone else do the assembly. Label your quilt blocks, working in rows or from the center out. Give all dimensions for each type of block and how many are needed of each color. Such a diagram will make the job easier for the assembler.

If you are doing the work yourself, you will need to make templates for each type of block. If you're using standard sizes, you can buy plastic or metal templates. Or you can make them from cardboard or sheets of thin plastic. If you're making your own, make sure they are even and straight and that you allow for ¼-inch seams.

Next, cut and piece your blocks. Precision is of utmost importance. Trace the template pattern on your fabric before cutting to ensure straight lines. To avoid fabric waste, cut the borders first. Each border strip should be cut in one continuous strip, unless the borders will be pieced. Then cut the smaller pieces. Keep the pieces sorted by color and shape.

Sew pieces together, block by block. Press seams open as you go. Join the blocks row by row. Then, join row to row.

Overlapped borders are the easiest. With right sides together, pin the lengthwise border strips to the quilt top. Machine stitch, leaving a ¼-inch seam allowance. Repeat with the widthwise border strips.

Mark the quilting or tufting pattern on quilt top. Since the individual blocks are the important thing in a friendship quilt, intricate quilting should be reserved for the joining strips and borders.

Make the lining by joining fabric as needed for width and length of your quilt. The lining can be in a coordinating color, a neutral, or one of the fabrics used in the quilt top.

Lay the interlining on the floor; remove any wrinkles. Place lining on top, face up. Baste or pin the two layers together, working from the center out according to the diagram. Turn the layers over so the lining is on the floor and interlining faces up. Smooth it out. Place pressed quilt top over the other two layers, making sure all layers are even at all four corners. Pin and baste through all three layers, starting in the center and working toward the edges. Do not trim the interlining or lining until the quilting is completed. Mount the layers on a quilting frame if you are going to use a frame.

Begin quilting in the center of the section you're working on, working out to the edges. This removes the wrinkles as you go. Quilt or tie your project according to the markings on quilt top.

To quilt, use a sharp needle and a single strand of cotton thread. Make a small knot in the end of thread. Insert needle through lining toward top. Tug gently on thread to pull knot through lining fabric, so it will be buried in the interlining. Take small, even stitches.

To trim and bind the quilt, you can either use coordinating bias tape or fabric used in the quilt. If using bias tape, pin the tape to the quilt top, right sides together. Start in the middle of a side. Sew it all around the quilt, keeping corners square. Grade seams. Fold the tape to the back; blindstitch it by hand.

You can make your own binding by cutting fabric into 2-inch wide strips joined together in a long strip measuring the quilt perimeter plus 1 or 2 inches. Attach it the same as you would the bias tape.

If large enough, the quilt lining can be used for binding. Trim the interlining to the quilt top. Trim the lining so it is 1½ or 2 inches larger than the quilt top on all sides. Bring the lining forward and pin to the top, folding under ⅜ inch as you go. Blindstich to the quilt top.

*

Wall Hangings • Quilting

Quilts make beautiful wall hangings, even for a church. They can warm up a basement, adding insulation to a cold wall. Because of their bulk, they also help deaden sound. An artful quilt can serve in place of a wall mural or be used as a room divider.

Quilts should be hung carefully—both for protection and to show them off. They should never be stapled or nailed to a wall.

DIRECTIONS: Cut a 1-by-2-inch strip of wood to the width of the quilt. Cut a 7-inch strip of muslin 4 inches longer than the wood. Place the wood in the center of the muslin. Wrap muslin around wood, allowing edges to overlap. Staple edges in place. Fold in ends; staple in place. The unstapled side is the front.

In the top of the wood strip, insert a screweye ¼ of the total distance from either side. Attach picture wire to screweyes.

Pin center of quilt to center of muslin-covered strip. Pin corners to ends of strip. Pin halfway between center and corners. Continue pinning in halves until pins are very closely spaced. (Instead of pinning, you can overcast the quilt binding to the muslin.) Let quilt hang loosely.

Friendship Quilt Diagram # 1

SIZE: 81¾ by 93½ inches.

MATERIALS: 2⅔ yards color #1, 44 inches wide; 6½ yards color #2, 44 inches wide; 5¼ yards lining fabric, 44 inches wide; batting; thread.

PIECES: Pattern pieces A, F, and G are all cut from color #2. Pieces B, C, D, E, H, and I are cut from color #1. The following measurements include ¼-inch seam allowance:

Piece A: 11¼ by 11¼ inches; 30 needed.
Piece B: 1½ by 11¼ inches; 24 needed.
Piece C: 1½ by 58¼ inches; 5 needed.
Piece D: 2½ by 62¼ inches; 2 needed.
Piece E: 2½ by 74 inches; 2 needed.
Piece F: 8¼ by 77¾ inches; 2 needed.
Piece G: 8¼ by 89½ inches; 2 needed.
Piece H: 2½ by 81¾ inches; 2 needed.
Piece I: 2½ by 93½ inches; 2 needed.

This diagram is intended to show how pieces fit together. Measurements represented in this diagram are not exact.

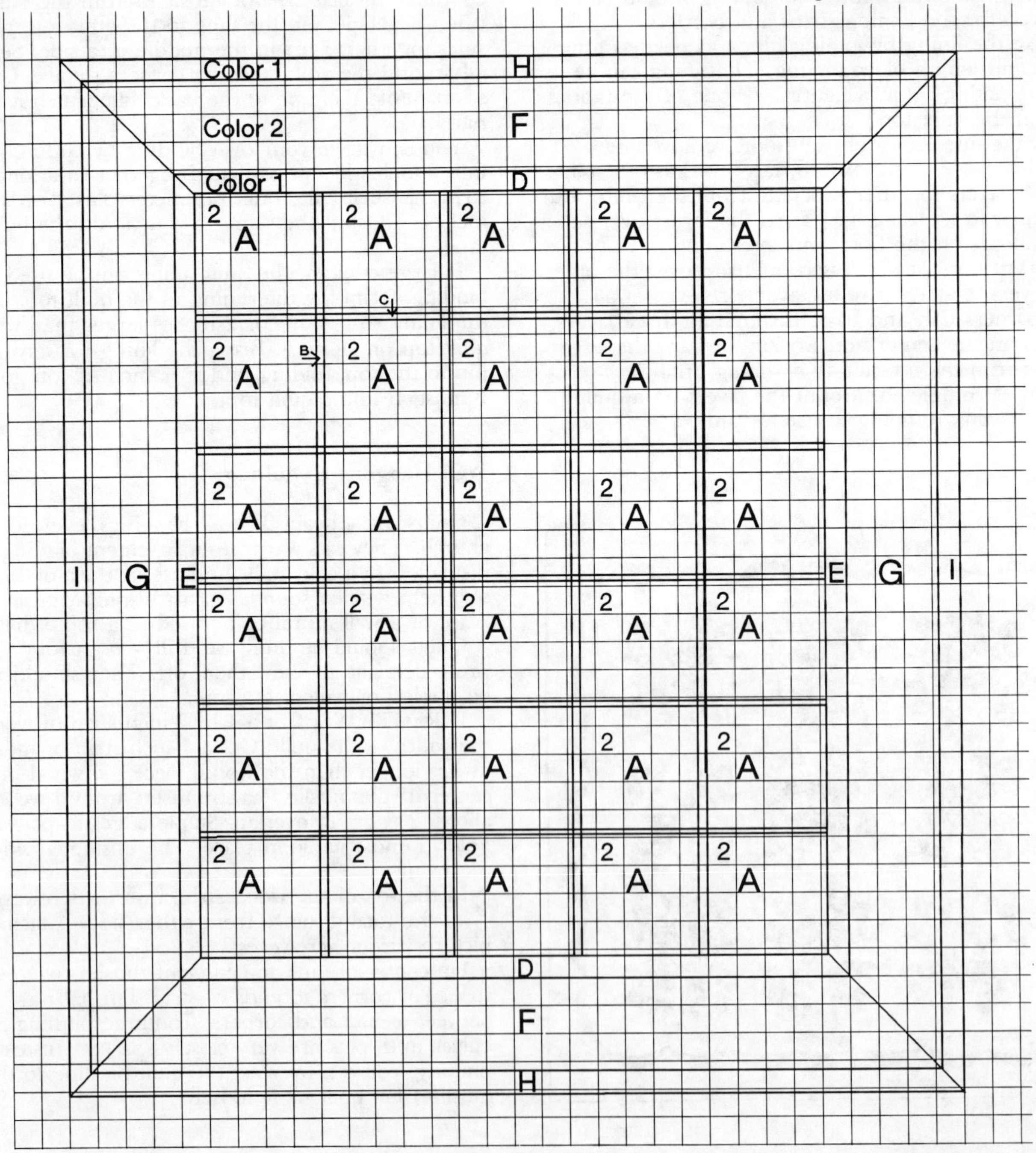

Friendship Quilt Diagram #2

SIZE: 81¾ by 93½ inches.

MATERIALS: About the same as for #1.

PIECES: Pattern pieces A, B, H, and I are cut from color #2. Pieces C, D, E, F, G, J, and K are cut from color #1. The following measurements include ¼-inch seam allowance:

Piece A: 35¾ by 46½ inches; 1 needed.
Piece B: 11¼ by 11¼ inches; 18 needed.
Piece C: 1½ by 11¼ inches; 18 needed.
Piece D: 1½ by 46½ inches; 2 needed.
Piece E: 1½ by 37½ inches; 2 needed.
Piece F: 2½ by 62¼ inches; 2 needed.
Piece G: 2½ by 74 inches; 2 needed.
Piece H: 8¼ by 77¾ inches; 2 needed.
Piece I: 8¼ by 89½ inches; 2 needed.
Piece J: 2½ by 81¾ inches; 2 needed.
Piece K: 2½ by 93½ inches; 2 needed.

This diagram is intended to show how pieces fit together. Measurements represented in this diagram are not exact.

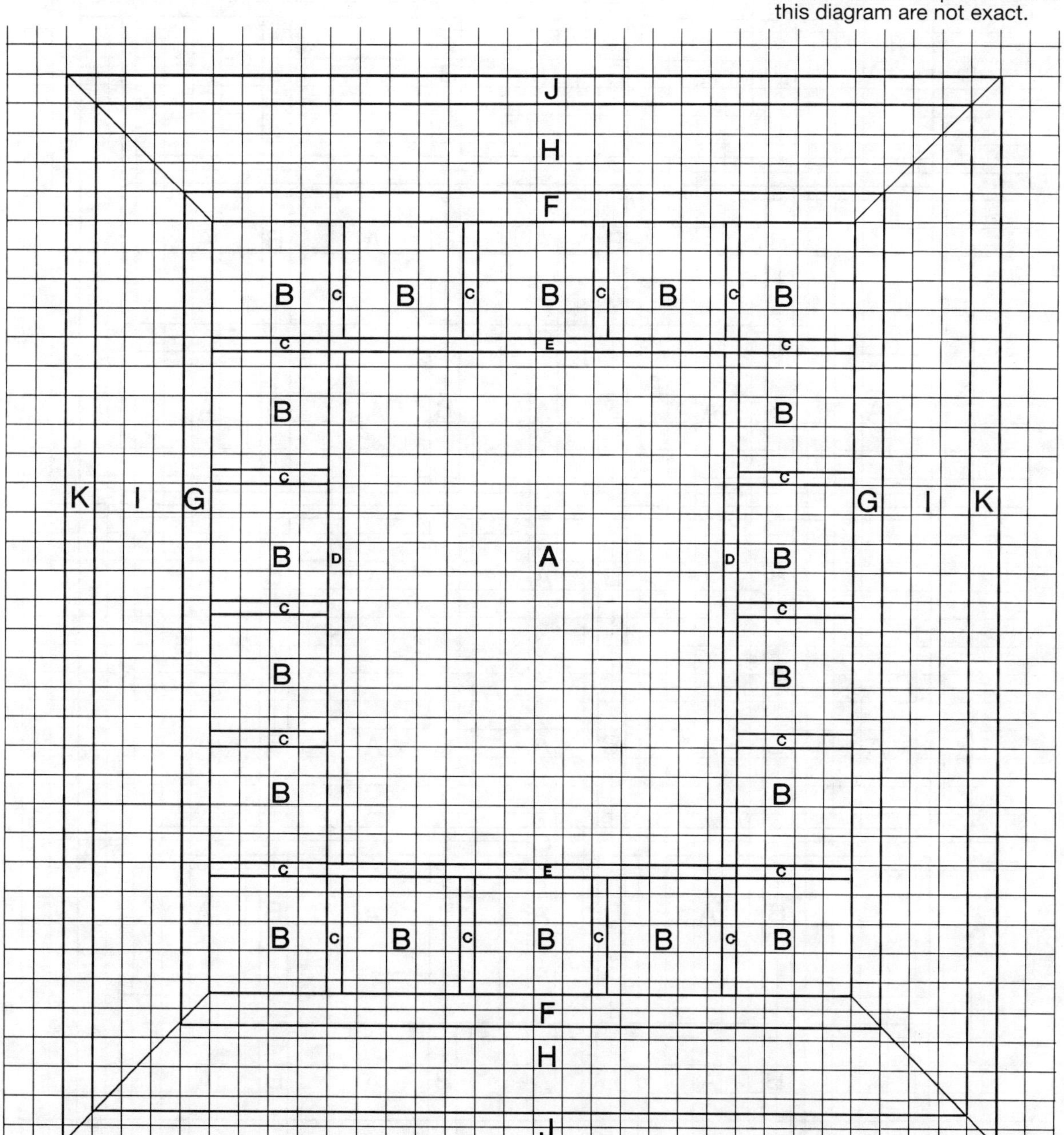

Friendship Quilt Diagram #3

SIZE: 71 by 97 inches

MATERIALS: Color #1 for borders and joining strips; color #2 for blocks.

PIECES: Pattern pieces B, C, D, and E should all be cut from color #1. Piece A should be cut from color #2. The following measurements include ¼-inch seam allowance:

Piece A: 11½ by 11½ inches; 35 needed.
Piece B: 2½ by 11½ inches; 28 needed.
Piece C: 2½ by 63½ inches; 6 needed.
Piece D: 4½ by 71½ inches; 2 needed.
Piece E: 4½ inches by 89½ inches; 2 needed.

This diagram is intended to show how pieces fit together. Measurements represented in this diagram are not exact.

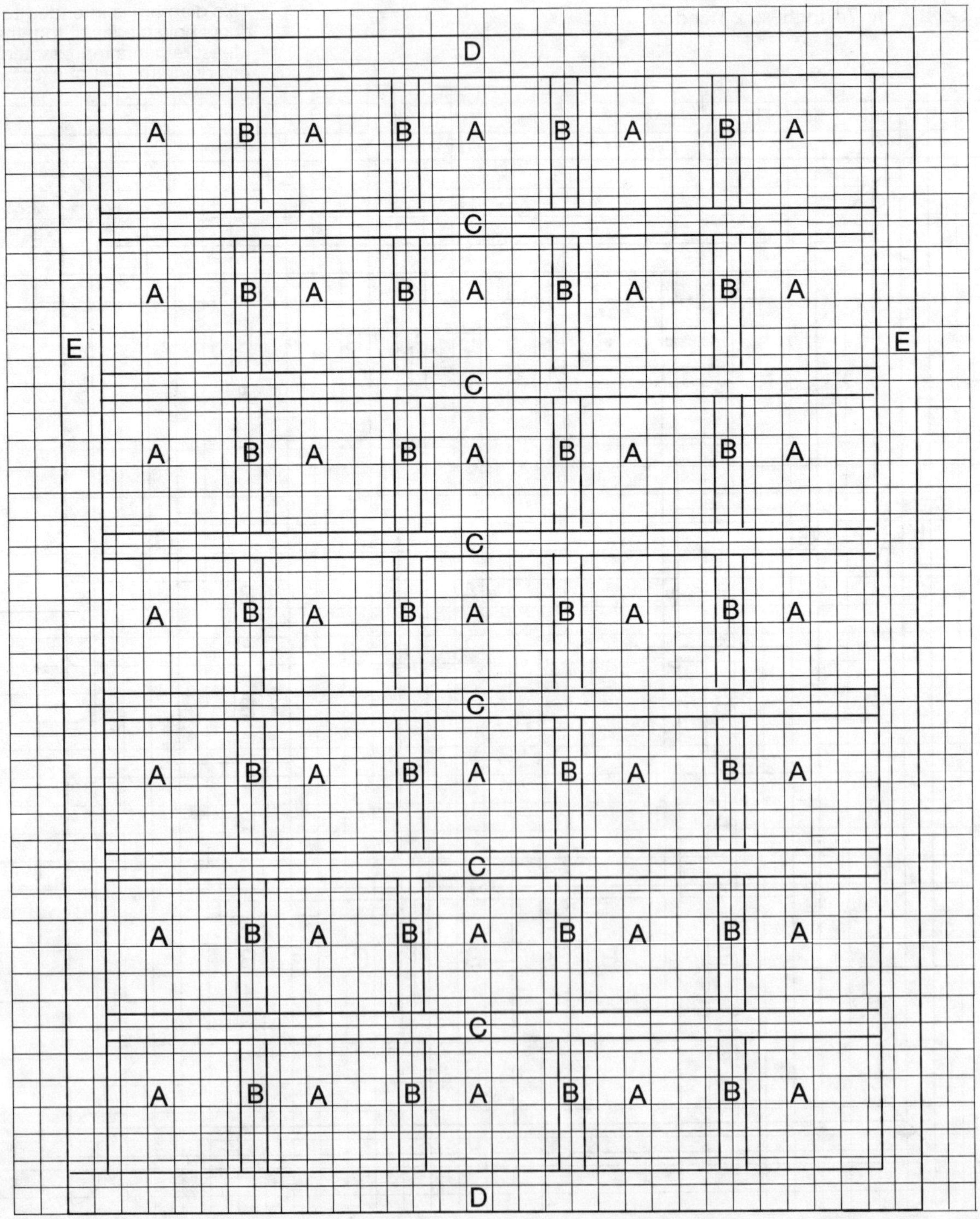

Friendship Quilt Diagram #4

SIZE: 63 by 78 inches

MATERIALS: Two different fabrics.

PIECES: Pattern piece A is cut from one fabric; all other pieces are cut from the other fabric. The following measurements include ¼-inch seam allowance:

Piece A: 12½ by 12½ inches; 20 needed.
Piece B: 3½ by 12½ inches; 15 needed.
Piece C: 3½ by 57½ inches; 4 needed.
Piece D: 3½ by 63½ inches; 2 needed.
Piece E: 3½ by 72½ inches; 2 needed.

This diagram is intended to show how pieces fit together. Measurements represented in this diagram are not exact.

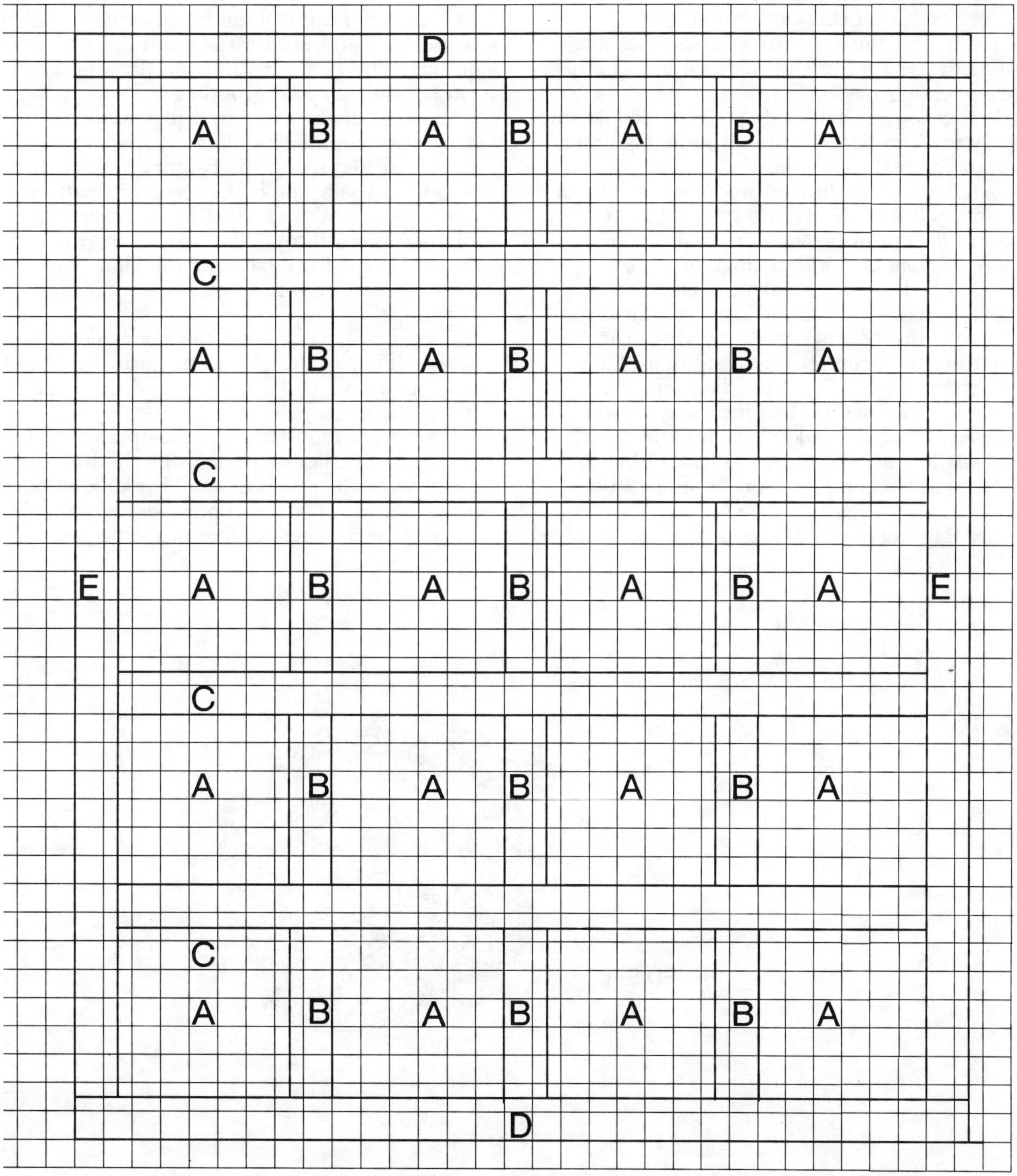

CREATING FOR THE BAZAAR

Typically, the church crafters have had one format in which to shine—the church bazaar. A bazaar is often used to fatten church budgets, fund a special project, or help finance a specific group in the church.

Even if your church is one that looks askance at selling things in the Lord's house, you could get the crafters in your congregation together outside the church for fund-raising benefits for accident victims, families hit by a personal disaster, for a mission project, or for a local charity. Though not sanctioned by the church, such a fund-raiser still allows you to use your talents to reach out to others in a loving, caring way.

In addition to the usual craft projects, people who frequently work in bazaars offered some big-ticket suggestions for real "hot sellers."

Crocheted and hand-beaded wedding dresses for Barbie dolls sell for $25 and up in some parts of the country (beautiful patterns are available in *McCalls Needlework & Crafts* catalogue).

Crocheted bed dolls are making a big comeback with intricate patterns available at most craft stores. Use unique yarns, beading, laces, ribbons, parasols, and tiny roses to create one-of-a-kind dolls. Such dolls sell from $25 to $75, depending on what part of the country you live in. Besides being a good bazaar seller, the dolls could cheer up a little girl who has just lost her mommy, has had all her toys destroyed in a disaster, or suffers from a chronic illness.

Another big money-maker is a dollhouse made from a kit, available at craft stores for about $20. Stencil the floors and walls or wallpaper the walls. A book of dollhouse wallpaper is available at many bookstores in the hobbies and crafts section. Add miniature curtains, crocheted rugs, and a tiny wreath or two. The unfurnished dollhouse could earn $200 dollars at a Christmas bazaar.

To furnish the dollhouse, check into miniature furniture kits. The major pattern companies offer patterns for a variety of dollhouse curtains, linens, and pillows. Lace tablecloths, placemats, afghans, potholders, and even carpets can be crocheted quickly. The furniture and coordinating accessories can be sold in room groupings.

Wooden ducks, cows, and pigs; unusual macrame hangings; handmade doll cradles; wooden shelves; and other items with the country look are also big favorites. Again, the crafts section in pattern catalogs can offer a wealth of ideas for whimsical stuffed animals, fanciful toys, and a vast array of home decor. Many of the patterns will allow you to create the expensive country accessories available in elite gift shops.

Photographers can also use their talents at a bazaar. They could take scenic pictures, have them enlarged to 8 × 10 (or larger), and then matte and frame them.

Or the photographer can set up an area to take photos of families or perhaps of children on Santa's lap at your Christmas bazaar. For unique portraits, provide a variety of costumes—either biblical, fanciful, or antique—and appropriate settings.

CROCHETED SACHET

**

Sachets • Crochet

Sweet-smelling sachets are quick and easy to make. They could be sold at bazaars as gift items, in sets of six, or as Christmas tree ornaments.

MATERIALS: Cotton crochet thread in natural or white; size 8 steel crochet hook; potpourri; miniature rose made of ribbon; needle and thread or hot glue gun.

DIRECTIONS: Chain (ch) 36.

Row 1: Single crochet (sc) in second ch from hook (first 2 ch count as 1 sc), sc in each ch across. Ch 1; turn.

Row 2: Sc in first sc and in each sc across. Ch 1; turn.

Repeat Row 2 until piece measures 8 inches. On last row, do not end off. Fold work in half, widthwise, to make a 4-inch square. Ch 2. Sew edges together by working sc across ends with a sc in each sc. Work 3 sc in corner sc. Turn work. Continue sc down side, working 1 sc at end of each row; 3 sc in corner. Turn; sc evenly down foldline; 3 sc in corner. Before closing up final side, fill sachet with potpourri. Continue sc down last side, working 1 sc at end of each row. Work 1 sc in corner; slip stitch in top of ch 2.

Edging, Rnd 1: Ch 3; work 4 double crochet (dc) in same stitch as slip stitch; sc in next stitch; (5 dc in next stitch, sc in next stitch) all the way around, spacing as needed so 5 dc are worked in middle stitch on each corner. At end of round, slip stitch in top of ch 3. Slip stitch in next 2 dc; ch 2 (counts as sc).

Rnd 2: Skip next 2 dc; 5 dc in sc; (skip 2 dc, sc in next dc, skip 2 dc, 5 dc in sc) all the way around. Slip stitch in top of ch 2; ch 3.

Rnd 3: 4 dc in same stitch as slip stitch; skip 2 dc; sc in next dc; skip 2 dc; (5 dc in sc, skip 2 dc, sc in next dc, skip 2 dc) all the way around. Slip stitch in top of ch 3. End off, weave in loose ends.

Finishing: Glue or tack ribbon rose in center front of sachet.

*

Fabric Sachet • Sewing

Even if you don't crochet, sachets are easy to make. Use your imagination to create a patchwork, embroidered, stenciled, or appliqued sachet. Another possibility would be to use scraps of a lace-covered satin or tricot. Trim with ruffled lace, short fringe, or cording.

MATERIALS: Scrap of fabric; potpourri; 18½ inches of trim; thread.

DIRECTIONS: Cut two 4¼-inch squares of fabric. With right sides together and using ¼-inch seam allowance, seam all edges, leaving a 2-inch opening for turning and stuffing. Turn right side out. Fill with potpourri. Slip stitch opening. Sew trim around the edges, mitering at the corners.

**

Mesh Scarf • Crochet

Luxurious scarves to fend off the winter wind are another great bazaar item. They also make nice gifts for people in need. A scarf done on a large hook with a novelty boucle yarn works up quickly while looking expensive. Made in voluminous proportions, it can be folded or softly draped to keep out the coldest chill.

SIZE: 24 by 103 inches

MATERIALS: Seven 1¾-ounce skeins of a soft boucle yarn, knitting worsted weight; size K crochet hook; large tapestry needle.

DIRECTIONS: Ch 88.

Row 1: Dc in 4th ch from hook, first 3 ch count as 1 dc; (ch 1, skip 1 ch, dc in next ch) 42 times; dc in last ch. Ch 3; turn.

Row 2: Dc in second dc; (ch 1, dc in next dc) 42 times; dc in last dc. Ch 3; turn.

Repeat Row 2 until scarf measures desired length. On last row, ch 2 instead of 3.

Edging: Sc in second dc; (sc in ch space, sc in dc) 42 times; sc in last dc. End off. Join yarn to other end. Ch 2, sc in second dc; (sc in ch space, sc in dc) 42 times; sc in last dc. End off. Weave in all loose ends.

*

Bandana Scarf • Craft

One of the recent arrivals on the wearable craft scene is an old-time favorite—dressed up. Bandanas are cropping up in a variety of wearable accessories, from beaded bibs to necklace-type scarves. The latter are simple to make and are good sellers at bazaars.

MATERIALS: Bandana-sized scarf; two 1¼-inch long wooden barrel beads; a heart-shaped wooden disk; ¼-inch drill and bit; 10-inch long leather thong; two small plastic butterfly-shaped beads; four small round plastic beads in one color and four in a coordinating color; hot glue gun; small-tipped paint brush; and tole paints in colors to coordinate with the bandana.

DIRECTIONS: Drill two ¼-inch diameter holes in center of heart. (The holes should be about ½ inch apart, horizontally.) Paint wooden beads and heart in a neutral color to complement scarf. Let dry. In coordinating colors, tole paint flowers, hearts, bows, etc. on front of beads and heart disk. Let dry.

Fold bandana in half, diagonally. Starting at pointed end, fold lengthwise in 2½-inch folds. Thread a barrel bead on each end, pushing up until beads are about 6 inches from ends. Twist beads so decorated fronts face the same direction.

Twist one bandana end tightly. Thread from back of heart through one hole. Thread that end back through the other hole, pulling about 2½ inches through to the back. Pull taut. Repeat with the other end of the bandana, but reverse the order of holes. With hot glue gun, securely glue bandana where it enters the holes on the back side of the heart, but keep ends free.

Thread one of each color plastic bead on each end of the leather thong. Thread a butterfly bead on each end. Thread the remaining plastic beads in each end. Tightly knot the end of each thong.

Tie the two ends of bandana together. Place center of thong over the tie. Tightly knot bandana ends over thong to hold thong securely in place.

This can be worn as a necklace or kerchief. You could create new looks by varying the beads, color combination, and middle disk.

LENDING A HELPING HAND

Perhaps nowhere are a crafter's skills more needed than in the outreach ministry of the church. In these days of soup kitchens, homeless families, and dire poverty, a simple handcrafted gift could literally make the difference between life or death for someone.

A warm lap robe, shawl, afghan, or slippers for someone living in a shelter for the homeless; homebaked bread or cinnamon rolls delivered to the local soup kitchen or rescue mission; dolls and doll clothes or wooden trucks and trains for children in hospitals—the gift you give would at the very least brighten someone's life.

A church in the northern Pennsylvania hill country makes numerous quilts from fabric scraps. When a family is "burned out" (a frequent occurrence in the area because of faulty chimneys and wood stoves), the church delivers a quilt to the fire victims. This tradition serves the practical purpose of keeping someone warm and is a ray of hope to the recipient in his devastation.

Following the Teton Dam disaster in Idaho several years ago, the Interfaith Disaster Task Force delivered blankets, quilts, and clothing to the hundreds of families who were left homeless. Just knowing someone cared and shared their burden brought new hope and energies to those who had lost absolutely everything to the swirling flood waters. The encouragement dawned again six months later when Christmas gifts, trees, and handmade ornaments poured in from across the country to replace those lost earlier in the flood.

Even if a disaster occurs earlier in the year, Christmas has a way of making the victims relive it and wonder if the holidays will ever be the way they used to be. This is especially true of people who have lost a loved one during the year or who have gone through a messy divorce. It knocks the spirit out of them, depriving them of the energy it takes to decorate or celebrate the holidays.

Christmas is a time to seek out those who are grieving or hurting and touch them with a homemade gift. Such a gift means far more than a purchased one, because the recipient knows you were thinking of him every minute you put into that gift.

Helping others is not new to this generation. One of the main premises of Christianity is to minister, in all ways, to others. The book of Acts tells of a disciple in Joppa named Dorcas, "who was always doing good and helping the poor" (Acts 9:36). Dorcas is well-known to most Sunday school children, who have seen pictures of her sewing coats for the poor.

The gift of sewing can be a ministry that deserves to be right up there with preaching, choir directing, and teaching. And it certainly takes no less skill and dedication than the "Big 3."

*

Lap Robes • Sewing

Lap robes for the elderly are simple and inexpensive to make using discarded sheets for backing, worn blankets for batting, and a pieced, appliqued, embroidered, or other decorative top.

DIRECTIONS: Cut a twin sheet in half, widthwise. Using the half sheet as a pattern, cut the blanket and top fabric. Layer the blanket between the sheet and the top, sandwich-style, and simply tie the materials together as you would tie a quilt. Sew wide seam binding tape around all edges.

The resulting lap robe will be nice and warm and guaranteed to make an elderly patient in a wheelchair toasty and comfortable. Besides being a creature comfort, it will remind that person that he has not been forgotten.

*

Costumes • Sewing

The talents of a person handy with needle and thread can be used within the church as well. A church in southern Idaho has a gorgeous array of nativity costumes, with an entire wardrobe to outfit tiny tots, juniors, teens, and adults. Whatever group plans to do a Christmas pageant has only to go to the wardrobe closet and select a set in the proper size range.

Compliments of a seamstress in the congregation, the costumes were made from inexpensive, washable polyester bought on sale at a remnant house. Old sheets, cotton, or satin fabrics work well, too. Burlap, ropes, heavily textured shawls, and scarves also can be used.

Patterns for nativity costumes are available at fabric stores, but an experienced seamstress could make a pattern. A simple T-shape pullover costume with only a few seams makes an excellent Palestinian robe.

MATERIALS: Use a coarse fabric for the shepherds and Joseph, blue for Mary's, white satin for the angels, and a rich-looking satin, brocade, velour, or velveteen for the wise men. Using 60-inch wide fabric eliminates the need for extra seams. Make coordinating tie sashes, sleeveless over-robes, and headdresses. Adorn the wisemen's costumes with elegant braid or sequins. Use newspaper or newsprint (available at most newspaper offices by the roll end) for the pattern or mark the pattern directly on the fabric.

DIRECTIONS: To fit the pattern to the actor, measure from center of chest to wrist. (This measurement will be the width of the pattern at the top.) Take another measurement from center of waist to side of waist and add at least 3 more inches for freedom of movement and ½-inch seam allowance. (This measurement will be the width of the pattern under the sleeve section.) For length, measure from shoulder to ankle, add 1 inch for hem and shoulder seam. This will be the length of the pattern. To determine yardage, multiply the length measurement by 2 and divide by 36.

For an adult pattern, the sleeve section should be 12 inches deep. A child's pattern would need only about 8-inch deep sleeves.

Fold fabric in half, lengthwise. Place center line of pattern on fold; pin pattern in place. Cut out fabric. Repeat, as you will need two fabric pieces for each garment. Put fabric pieces right sides together and stitch at shoulder and upper arm seams. (All seams should be ½-inch from edge.) Starting 8 inches from bottom of each side, stitch side seams, continuing into underarm seams. Narrow hem bottom, sleeves, neckline, and walking slits.

Following the same directions, make sleeveless over-robes out of coordinating fabric. By creating a variety of costume pieces, you can provide your church with the costumes needed for Christmas programs, biblical skits or plays.

*

Choir Robes • Sewing

To get your church cherubs into the sing of things, make them circular capes to give them that angelic appearance and make them feel like a grown-up choir. Again, sheets make for an inexpensive, easy-to-care-for fabric, but you could use a white fabric in a cotton/polyester blend.

MATERIALS: Newspaper or newsprint for pattern; marker; scissors; 1 yard white fabric for each cape; ⅓ yard red fabric for bow; thread.

DIRECTIONS: Make pattern; cut out. Fold fabric in half, lengthwise. Pin pattern in place, putting center back on fold. Cut. Narrow hem neckline, around bottom of cape and front center opening. Sew on a snap or Velcro fastener at center front neck.

Pin pattern pieces for bow and knot on red fabric; cut. With right sides together, fold bow in half, widthwise. Stitch around three edges, using a ½-inch seam allowance. Leave a small opening for turning. Trim seam allowance. Turn bow right side out. Slip stitch opening. Following fold lines on pattern, fold bow—seam should be centered in back. Press.

With right sides together, fold knot piece in half, lengthwise. Stitch ½-inch seam; trim seam. Turn right side out. Following fold lines on pattern, fold knot—seam should be centered in back. Press. With front together, fold knot in half, lengthwise. Stitch ½-inch seam across ends; trim. Turn right side out. Slip bow through knot, centering knot. Tack in place. Tack completed bow onto top right corner of cape, covering fastener.

A creative seamstress could also make satin stoles for the adult choir, changing the colors to match the liturgical season. A seamstress at an Idaho church made the pastoral stoles for her minister, saving him the expense. Such stoles could employ elaborate embroidery.

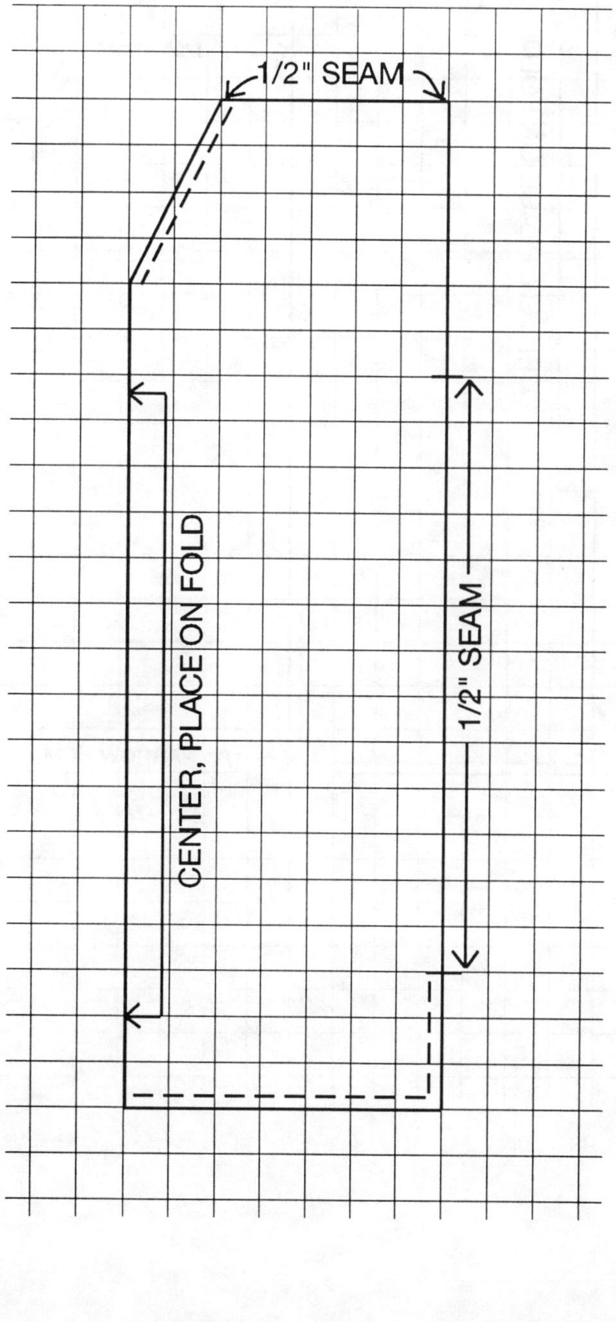

OVER ROBE PATTERN
Make 6 to10 inches shorter than robe.

(1 square = 2 inches) — — — narrow hem

BASIC ROBE PATTERN

(1 square = 2 inches) — — — narrow hem

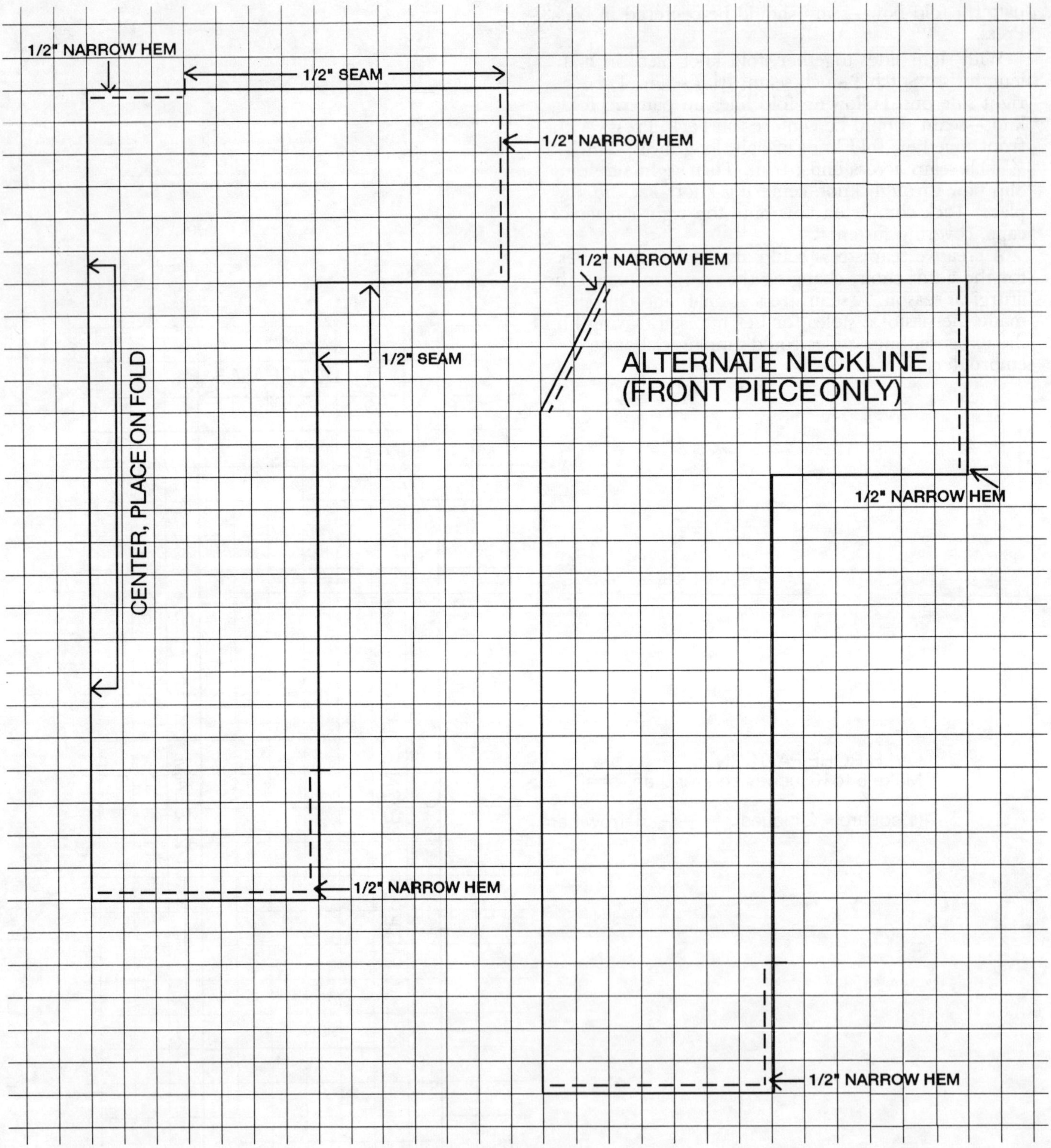

PATTERN FOR CIRCULAR CHOIR ROBE AND BOW

(1 square = 1 inch) — — — narrow hem ······· seam line

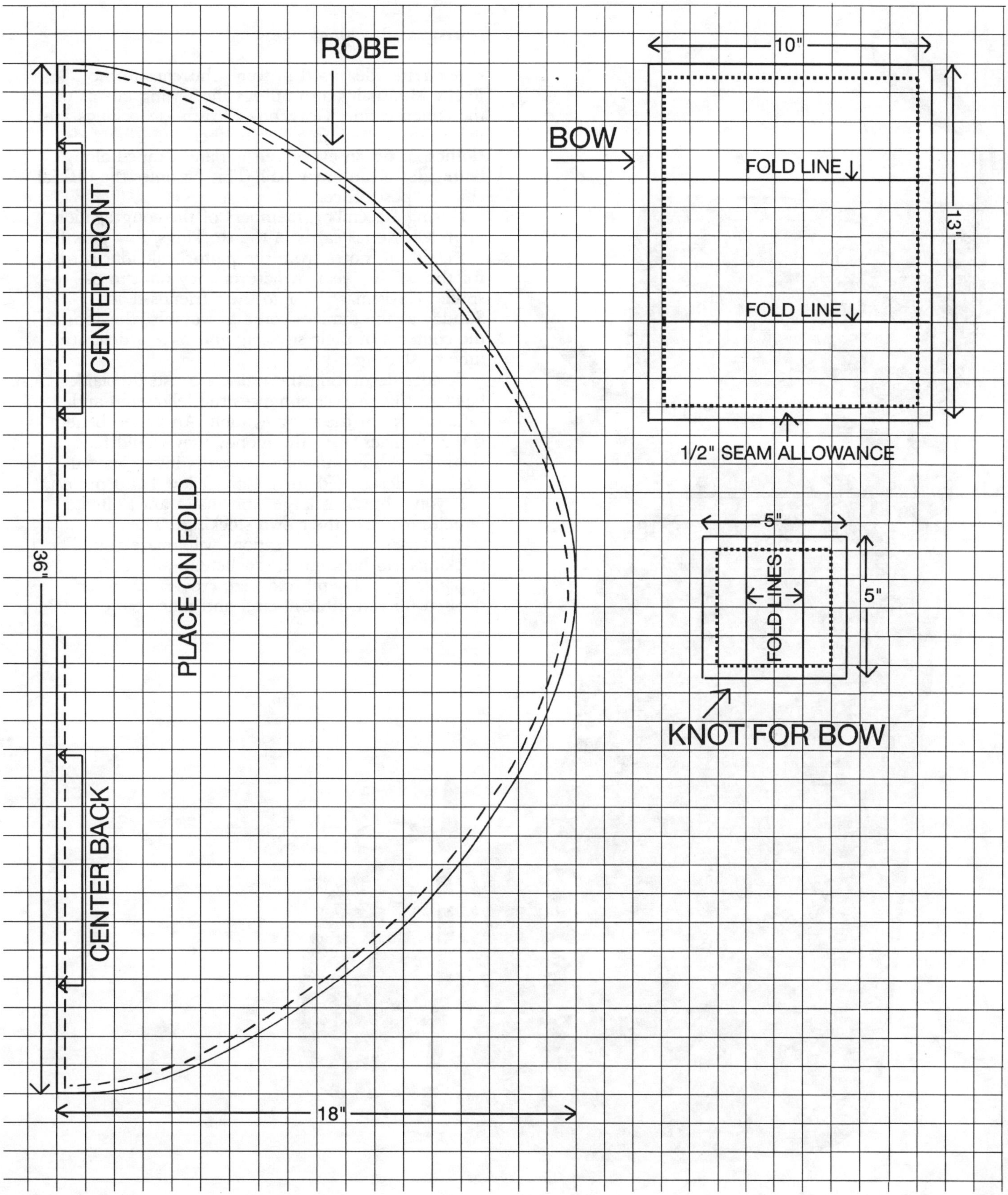

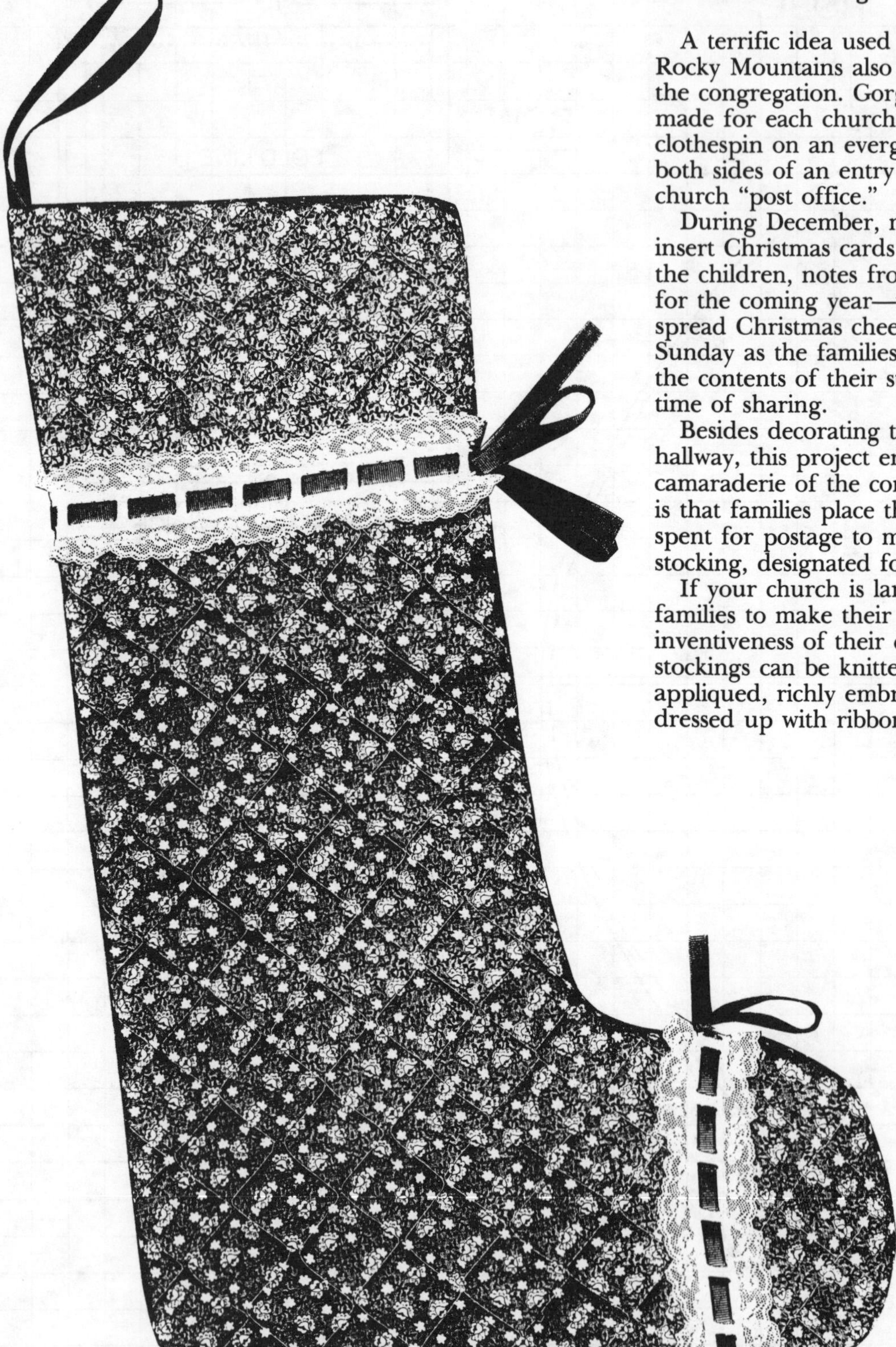

*

Christmas Stockings • Sewing

A terrific idea used in some churches in the Rocky Mountains also utilizes the sewing talents of the congregation. Gorgeous Christmas stockings are made for each church family, then hung by a clothespin on an evergreen garland draped along both sides of an entry hall. This becomes the official church "post office."

During December, members of the congregation insert Christmas cards in the stockings, tiny gifts for the children, notes from the pastor, calendar cards for the coming year—whatever they want to use to spread Christmas cheer to their friends. Each Sunday as the families come to worship, they empty the contents of their stocking and have a delightful time of sharing.

Besides decorating the walls of a usually blank hallway, this project enhances the fellowship and camaraderie of the congregation. An added benefit is that families place the money they would have spent for postage to mail the cards into a special stocking, designated for a Goodfellow Fund project.

If your church is large, you may want to invite families to make their own stockings. The inventiveness of their creations will amaze you. The stockings can be knitted, crocheted, quilted, appliqued, richly embroidered, cross-stitched, or dressed up with ribbon, lace, and fancy buttons.

Missionary Cabinet

While the missionary barrel of yesteryear is no longer with us, many churches have a missionary cabinet or closet where missionaries preparing to leave for an overseas assignment can select items they need. The cabinet also provides necessities for foreign missionaries who have just returned home on furlough.

The most popular items in a missionary supply cabinet are sheets, embroidered dish towels, cobbler aprons, lightweight bedspreads, children's birthday cards, plus staples such as shampoo, crayons, dental floss, deodorant. The cabinet can also include craft books and magazines, handmade potholders, doilies, tablerunners, wall hangings—anything that can bring a touch of home and the well wishes of those praying for missionaries.

Some groups like to send "relief packages" to their missionaries. Because of postage and customs in other countries, such packages can cost far more than they're worth. Usually, the missionary has to pay officials to receive the package. Many missionaries have stories of paying precious money to get a package, not knowing what was in the box. Opening it with growing anticipation, they found only outdated Sunday school materials, threadbare clothing, and, yes, even used teabags.

Giving to God means giving our best. When we share with God's people, we should also give our best—not our throw-aways or garage sale refuse.

If your group wants to send something to a foreign missionary, check with the missionary first to see if he'll have any trouble with customs. A small gift that could be included in a letter also would be appreciated. If you are good with a camera, take some artsy snapshots of scenic landmarks, new developments in the community, or the aftermath of a local disaster. Missionaries from the area would appreciate these pictures of home.

Money Tree • Craft

Some churches set up a gift tree for the holidays. A large, bare tree branch is set in a container and secured with sand or stones. Spray paint the tree and container with gold, silver, copper, or a bright metallic paint.

If you're using the tree as an outreach ministry, check with an area homeless shelter, children's home, jail, or elderly care center for sizes or wish lists of the people at those places. Each individual's list is anonymously posted on a small card and numbered. The organizer keeps the master, number-coded list.

Each church family selects a card, purchases a gift from the list, numbers it, and places it under the tree. Just before Christmas, the organizer matches the gifts with the master list and delivers the packages.

If anonymity is not important, names could be placed on the cards instead of numbers.

The same tree could be used as a money tree as a special gift for the pastor, missionary, or other person your group wishes to honor. Ask guests to hang their cash gifts on the tree with paper clips, set it in the center of your party table, and present it to the honoree at the appropriate time.

When God needed Moses to lead his people into the Promised Land, he asked a simple question: "What is that in your hand?"

Whatever is in YOUR hand, be it artist's brush, crochet hook, knitting or sewing needle, woodworking tool, hot glue gun, camera, or flower, it can be used to glorify God, beautify your church, and make someone's life happier.

Don't keep your talent sitting idle on a pew!